THE CERTIFICATION SERIES

Start Powerboating Right!

The national standard for quality on-the-water instruction

Published by the UNITED STATES SAILING ASSOCIATION   Copyright © 2003 by the UNITED STATES SAILING ASSOCIATION
ISBN 0-9719593-2-3.   Printed in the United States of America
UNITED STATES SAILING ASSOCIATION, P.O. Box 1260, 15 Maritime Drive, Portsmouth, RI 02871-0907

Introduction

A Need for On-the-Water Training

Boating can be enjoyed in so many ways – waterskiing, fishing, exploring, cruising to different destinations, and best of all, spending a day on the water with family and friends. As more people discover the fun of boating, our waterways are becoming more crowded and more challenging. As with any activity, accidents do happen. Government statistics show that the vast majority (eighty-four percent) of serious boating accidents involve operators who had not completed a boating course.

This clearly highlights the importance of acquiring the necessary skills and knowledge to operate your boat safely and proficiently. While information in this book will help you become a more knowledgeable operator, it is not a substitute for hands-on instruction. Like learning to drive a car – you have to do it. The best way is to take an on-the-water powerboating course taught by a certified instructor.

Courtesy EdgeWater Powerboats

In conjunction with this book, the United States Sailing Association has developed an effective on-the-water training program to provide powerboat operators with the necessary skills and knowledge to safely and enjoyably operate their boats. Based on the collective experience of state agencies, the U.S. Coast Guard Academy, the U.S. Naval Academy, and other respected marine institutions, the program is designed to teach the essentials of boathandling, seamanship and safety in a clear and enjoyable style.

David Forbes photo

Hands-on, on-the-water courses taught by certified powerboat instructors are becoming available at an increasing number of community boating centers, schools, marinas and boating clubs. For more information on the program and participating organizations, go to *www.uspowerboating.com*

Courtesy EdgeWater Powerboats

Cover photo courtesy EdgeWater Powerboats

Contents

1. The Powerboat

KEY CONCEPTS
▶ Types of boats ▶ How a prop & jet work
▶ Parts of a boat ▶ Engine controls

If it had been possible to come up with the perfect powerboat design, all powerboats would look nearly alike. However, there is an infinite variety of types and sizes aimed at fulfilling different boating activities.

Displacement Boats

Displacement hulls create a bow wave as they push through the water. When the hull is trapped between a wave at the bow and another at the stern, it has reached its maximum speed.

Generally, boats with displacement hulls always move "through" the water at slow to moderate speeds rather than riding on top of the water. As they increase in speed, they develop waves at their bow (front end), along the sides and at the stern (back end). As they continue to increase speed, the waves become larger and the distance between them lengthen until the hull becomes trapped between the large wave at its bow and another large one at its stern. At this point, the displacement hull has reached what is called *hull speed*. This is the maximum speed for this hull. One of the most familiar examples of a displacement hull at hull speed is a tugboat moving at maximum speed with its hull sunk low in the water with a large bow and stern wave. Characteristics of displacement hulls include:

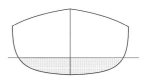

• Good maneuverability
• Speed limited by length (hull speed)
• Good ability to hold a course steered (directional stability)
• Good load carrying capacity
• Performance not greatly affected by load
• Good rough water handling
• May roll excessively when seas are coming sideways to the hull.

Planing Boats

A planing hull is designed to ride on top of the water once it has reached sufficient speed.

A planing hull behaves like a displacement hull at low speeds, forming waves at its bow (front end) and along the length of the hull. Upon reaching a certain speed it goes through a transition

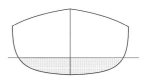

stage (*semi-displacement*) where it climbs the face of its bow wave. At this point the boat may become unstable, fuel consumption is high, and the operator may not be able to see over the raised bow. As the boat continues to accelerate it moves over the top of its bow wave, its bow levels off and the boat starts to plane along the top of the water with less wave making and using less fuel. But as the boat further increases its speed, wind and water friction on the hull also increase, causing a significant increase in fuel consumption. For most planing hulls the optimum fuel consumption with respect to distance traveled is achieved just as the boat has come comfortably on a plane. When a planing boat encounters waves, its ride can often become uncomfortable and at times even dangerously unstable. It may have to be slowed back to the displacement mode where it doesn't operate as well as its displacement cousin. There are several different shapes that can be used on a planing hull: flat, Vee and cathedral.

Flat-bottom Hulls. Basically most powerboat planing hulls are a variation of the flat-bottom hull. Their characteristics include:
• Good load carrying
• Below average in holding a course at
  low speeds — tend to slide or drift
• Inexpensive to construct
• Rough riding in waves

Flat bottom powerboats plane easily, but produce a bumpy ride in rough water.

Vee-bottom Hulls. The Vee-shaped hull, although again basically a flat bottom hull, has a pronounced Vee-shape to its bow where it cuts the water. Characteristics of this shape include:
• Good ability to hold a steered direction
  at speed
• Deeper Vees perform better in rough
  water
• Deep Vees tend to roll at rest

Vee-bottom powerboats have an angled bottom which improves ride and control in waves.

Cathedral Hulls. Cathedral hulls have two or three Vee shapes forward which turn into basically a flat hull aft. This gives greatly improved stability but with some of the unpleasant rough water ride as the pure flat bottom. Cathedral characteristics include:
• Good tracking at low speeds
• Good resistance to rolling even at rest
• Good load carrying capacity
• Uncomfortable at speed in rough water
• Tend toward lower freeboard

Cathedral hulls combine excellent stability and load carrying ability but produce a bumpy ride in waves.

Soft-Inflatable Hulls. These inflatables tend to be flat bottomed with the same rough and wet ride experienced in the pure flat-bottomed boat, perhaps even a little wetter. Their ability to hold a steered course (directional stability) is notoriously poor, particularly with any wind. The plastic impregnated

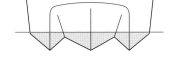

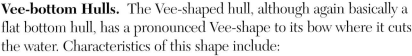

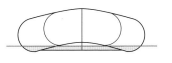

Soft inflatables are popular for their light weight and convenient storage, but can be difficult to steer and are vulnerable to puncture.

A rigid inflatable boat (RIB) combines the advantages of an inflatable with the control and seakindliness of a rigid Vee-bottom hull.

A multihull's narrow hulls and wide beam provide excellent stability and a smooth ride at the expense of maneuverability.

fabric can be sliced by sharp objects and is susceptible to the sun's ultraviolet radiation and chafe when dragging the hull up a rough beach or rubbing against a dock. In spite of these shortcomings they continue to be very popular due to their light weight, excellent buoyancy and stability at rest. Their characteristics include:
• Light weight and portable
• High stability
• Very high buoyancy
• High load carrying capacity
• Easily affected by wind
• Low ability to hold a steered course (sideslips or drifts)
• Rough, wet ride at speed
• Relatively short life
• Soft contact with other boats but vulnerable to damage

Rigid-Inflatable Boats (RIB's). These boats combine many of the advantages of the Vee-hull with the soft-inflatable. They have a rigid Vee-bottom (usually fiberglass) combined with the side buoyancy chambers of an inflatable. They have excellent sea keeping capabilities, good directional stability along with the buoyancy and initial stability of the inflatable. They are heavier than the soft-hull inflatable and do not fold and store as conveniently. Their characteristics include:

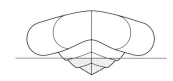

• Combined advantages of Vee-hull with inflatable
• Good ability to hold a steered course
• High buoyancy
• Exceptional seaworthiness in rough water
• High load carrying capacity
• Soft contact with other boats
• Not as vulnerable to damage on bottom of hull as soft inflatable

Multihulls

The catamaran hull configuration (two hulls) is used for houseboats, ferries and some race management boats in protected waters. Their characteristics include:
• Good ability to hold course at speed
• Good resistance to rolling
• Limited seaworthiness in bad weather
• Relatively shallow draft
• Cut through water rather than plane
• Large turning radius

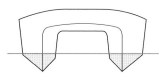

Personal Watercraft (PWC)

Personal Watercraft are frequently known by their common trade names, such as Jet Ski, Sea-Doo and WaveRunner. They use a water jet drive powered by a two-stroke or four-stroke gasoline inboard engine and are operated by a driver sitting on a saddle, or standing or kneeling. Characteristics include:
• Good agility and speed
• Good maneuverability except when rapidly reducing speed
• Driver may easily re-board after falling off
• No propeller or rudder to injure a person in the water

Parts of a Boat

The port side of a boat is the left side and the starboard side is the right side when looking forward. Later on in the Navigation Rules chapter you will learn that the sidelights, which are turned on for nighttime operation, are a red color on the port side and green color on the starboard side.

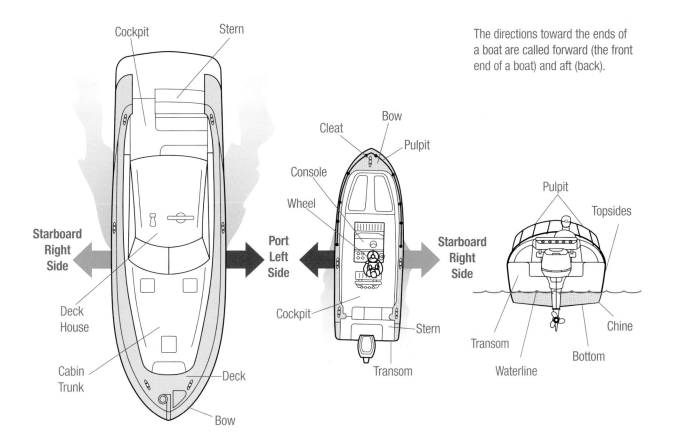

The directions toward the ends of a boat are called forward (the front end of a boat) and aft (back).

Propulsion: Prop or Jet?

Propulsion systems generally consist of two major components: an engine that produces power and a drive unit that propels the boat. There are two essential types of powerboat drive units:
• a propeller (*prop*)
• a water jet (jet drive)

How a Propeller Works

A rotating propeller produces thrust that moves the boat. When an engine is in forward gear, the thrust from the rotating propeller drives the boat forward. When the gear is shifted into reverse, the propeller turns in the opposite direction driving the boat backward. Because propeller blades are optimized for forward thrust, their performance in reverse is drastically reduced.

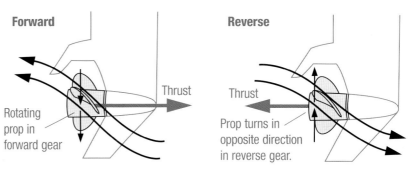

Forward

Rotating prop in forward gear

Thrust

Thrust generated from a rotating propeller drives a boat forward.

Reverse

Thrust

Prop turns in opposite direction in reverse gear.

A propeller rotating in the opposite direction drives a boat backward.

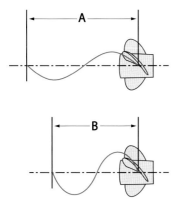

A low-pitch propeller (B) moves forward a smaller distance than a high-pitch propeller (A). The higher the pitch number, the greater the pitch (distance traveled per revolution).

When viewed from behind, if a propeller generates forward thrust by rotating in a clockwise direction, it is defined as a right-hand propeller. If it rotated in a counterclockwise direction in forward gear, it would be left-handed. Whether a propeller is right- or left-handed will become important when "prop walk" is discussed in Chapter 5.

Propeller size is defined by its *diameter* and *pitch*, and these factors have an important effect on the performance of a boat. Pitch is the distance that a propeller would move forward in a solid material in one full rotation. For example, a propeller with a 17-inch pitch would advance 17 inches. Since water is a fluid, the propeller would actually travel a distance less than 17 inches. Larger diameter propellers with less pitch that rotate at lower rpm (revolutions per minute) are used for slow-speed boats or towing vessels, while smaller propellers with higher pitch operating at higher rpm are used for high-speed boats. A wrong propeller size may result in engine overheating and/or a boat not reaching its designed speed.

Water flowing over the surfaces of a propeller blade produces a higher pressure on one side than the other. This pressure difference generates *lift* which results in thrust as well as a sideways force (torque). If pressure on the low-pressure side of the blades gets too low, bubbles of vaporized water (low temperature steam) will form on the blades. This bubbling action disrupts the water flow, causing the blades to lose lift and thrust and the engine to speed up. This phenomenon is called *cavitation*. When it occurs, reduce throttle and allow the propeller to "re-grip" the water. Cavitation can happen when too much throttle is applied too quickly, or if the propeller is damaged or not the right size.

How a Water Jet Works

A water jet has no propeller. Instead, water enters through an intake underneath the boat and is fed into a pump, which then accelerates it through a nozzle that produces thrust to move the boat.

Forward

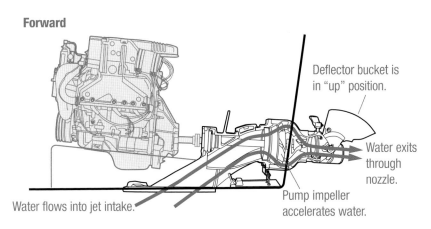

Deflector bucket is in "up" position.

Water exits through nozzle.

Pump impeller accelerates water.

Water flows into jet intake.

The jet of water exiting from the nozzle generates thrust to drive the boat forward. The nozzle can be pivoted sideways to turn the boat left or right.

Reverse

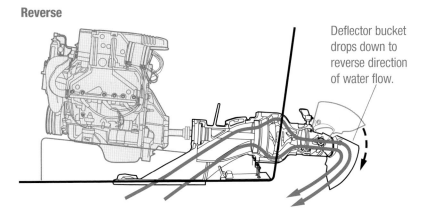

Deflector bucket drops down to reverse direction of water flow.

The deflector bucket reverses the jet of water that drives the boat backward.

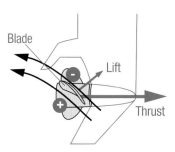

Blade

Lift

Thrust

As a propeller rotates through the water, the pressure on one side of the blades is higher ➕ than the other ➖, which generates lift and thrust.

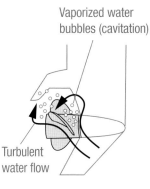

Vaporized water bubbles (cavitation)

Turbulent water flow

Cavitation causes the blades to lose lift and thrust.

**How a Combined Throttle/
Gearshift Lever Works**

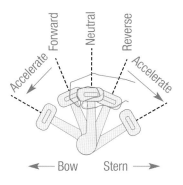

Bow ◄——   ——► Stern

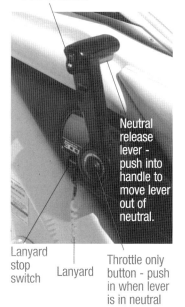

Trim/tilt button

Neutral release lever - push into handle to move lever out of neutral.

Lanyard stop switch

Lanyard

Throttle only button - push in when lever is in neutral position to increase throttle while in neutral.

Engine Controls

Remote throttle and gearshift controls are located at the steering stations, and the most common type for propeller-driven watercraft is the dual-function control with a single lever that combines throttle (speed) and gearshift (forward, neutral and reverse gears). It usually has a feature that will disengage the gearshift to allow you to increase the throttle when starting or warming up the engine. Another feature of many lever controls is not allowing the engine to be started unless the gearshift is in neutral. If nothing happens when the ignition key is turned on, check to make sure the lever is in the neutral position. When shifting from forward to reverse or reverse to forward, pause briefly in neutral (do a 1-2-3 count) to prevent possible damage to the gears.

Trim and Tilt Control

On stern drives and many outboard motors (typically above 25 hp) and jet drives, the angle of the drive unit to the boat can be changed (trimmed) while the boat is underway to achieve better performance. This is usually done by hydraulic rams, which are activated by a toggle button normally located on the throttle control lever. These hydraulic rams can also be used to tilt the drive out of the water when leaving the boat in the water or hauling out for storage or trailering. When operating in the trim range, the drive unit will move slowly, but once beyond the maximum UP trim position, the hydraulic speed will suddenly increase until the drive reaches its maximum tilt position. For more information on trim and how it affects a powerboat, see Chapter 5.

REVIEW QUESTIONS

1. The type of hull that moves "through" the water and has good rough water handling is a _____ hull. At higher speeds, it is the _____ hull that rises on top of the water, but may be uncomfortable in _____ water.
2. The optimum fuel consumption (best miles per gallon) for a boat on a plane occurs when just _____ on a _____.
3. Of the planing hull types, it is the _____ and _____ that give the best ride in rough water.
4. When a planing hull begins climbing its bow wave, it is in the _____ stage. At this point the boat may become _____ , fuel consumption is high, and _____ may be poor over the raised bow.
5. Propeller size is defined by its _____ and _____.

2. Outboard Motors

KEY CONCEPTS
▶ Two- & four-strokes
▶ Outboard motor parts
▶ Starting procedure
▶ Maintenance

Two-Stroke & Four-Stroke

Outboard motors can range in size from small two-horsepower (hp) units that weigh 25 pounds to massive 300 horsepower (hp) engines. They can be either *two-stroke* (two-cycle) or *four-stroke* (four-cycle). Two-stroke outboards use oil mixed into the gasoline to lubricate the engine. Each "compression" stroke of a piston is followed by a "power" stroke. As the power stroke comes to its end, a new mixture of gasoline/oil and air enters the cylinder and exhaust gases are forced out along with some of the new incoming mixture. These outboards have been regarded as serious polluters, but recent innovations, such as oil injection and the replacement of carburetors with fuel injection, have reduced pollution to a level almost comparable to the 4-stroke models.

Four-stroke outboards are lubricated by oil in the crankcase, similar to an automobile engine, and produce less pollution than two-stroke outboards. An "intake" stroke, which brings in a mixture of gasoline and air, precedes each "compression" stroke, which is followed by a "power" stroke. The "exhaust" stroke, which forces out the exhaust gases, completes the cycle and the next cycle starts again with the "intake" stroke.

As concerns about air and water pollution have increased, manufacturers have developed cleaner-running outboards. Some states have stringent pollution requirements for reservoirs and inland waters that may affect the use of your boat.

Parts of an Outboard Motor

Primer pumps are replacing the traditional choke in modern outboards. On electrically started engines, pushing in the key activates a "primer" pump that injects a small amount of fuel into the cylinder. More recently, manually activated primer pumps have been appearing on smaller outboards with manual pull-cord starting. At first glance these can be confused with a traditional choke knob, but they are usually accompanied by a decal on the face of the engine listing instructions for use. Manual primer pump knobs must be pulled out and then pushed back in to inject the fuel. Some retract automatically

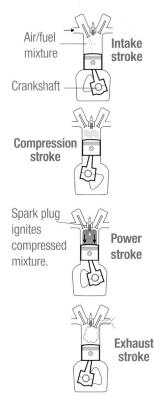

Compression stroke   **Power stroke**

ABOVE: A two-stroke engine fires once every revolution of the crankshaft.

BELOW: A four-stroke engine fires once every second revolution of the crankshaft.

Air/fuel mixture   **Intake stroke**

Crankshaft

Compression stroke

Spark plug ignites compressed mixture.   **Power stroke**

Exhaust stroke

while others must be pushed. If left out, the engine will not start. A traditional choke reduces the air supply in the carburetor, which enriches (increases the proportion of fuel) the fuel-air mixture that enters the cylinder, making the mixture easier to ignite. The choke control is pulled out to reduce or close the air supply.

Tilt lock-release lever appears on small outboards without an electric-hydraulic powered trim/tilt control. The lever is in the "release" position when operating in forward gear, which allows the

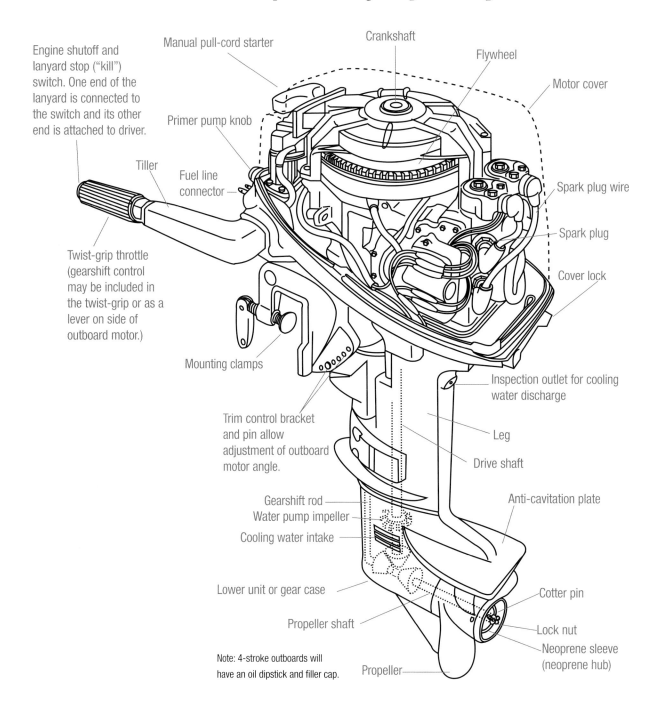

Engine shutoff and lanyard stop ("kill") switch. One end of the lanyard is connected to the switch and its other end is attached to driver.

Manual pull-cord starter

Crankshaft

Flywheel

Motor cover

Primer pump knob

Spark plug wire

Tiller

Fuel line connector

Spark plug

Cover lock

Twist-grip throttle (gearshift control may be included in the twist-grip or as a lever on side of outboard motor.)

Mounting clamps

Inspection outlet for cooling water discharge

Leg

Drive shaft

Trim control bracket and pin allow adjustment of outboard motor angle.

Anti-cavitation plate

Gearshift rod
Water pump impeller
Cooling water intake

Lower unit or gear case

Cotter pin

Lock nut

Propeller shaft

Neoprene sleeve (neoprene hub)

Note: 4-stroke outboards will have an oil dipstick and filler cap.

Propeller

outboard to kick up if it hits an underwater object. It must be placed in the "lock" position before shifting into reverse to prevent the outboard from tilting up.

Twist-grip throttle and gearshift. For outboards with a separate gearshift lever on the side of the motor, the twist grip throttle will usually have a shift position marked on it to which the throttle should be set before shifting the lever into forward, neutral or reverse so as to prevent serious damage to the outboard.

Shear pins and safety sleeves. All outboards have a designed weak link between the propeller and the propeller shaft to protect the engine and drive train if the propeller hits an object. Most outboards use a neoprene sleeve (neoprene hub) that is bonded to the propeller hub. When impact occurs, the bonding is broken, which protects the outboard. Although the bond has failed, there is usually enough friction in the neoprene hub to allow the engine to turn the propeller very slowly, often enough to return to safety. The propeller must then be removed and repaired. Smaller outboards may use a soft metal pin called a shear pin, which will break upon impact. Once the pin is sheared the propeller will no longer turn and it must be removed to replace the shear pin.

Outboard Inspection
- Outboard controls operate smoothly.
- Propeller blades, neoprene sleeve or shear pin are intact.
- Cooling water intake is clear.
- Oil level (applies to four-stroke or two-stroke with separate oil tank); add oil if indicated.
- Fuel tank level; add if indicated.
- Condition of fuel line (no cracks or sponginess) and connections.
- Any leaks in fuel system or gasoline odor in bilges.
- Condition of battery cables (no cracks, abrasion or frayed wire) and battery (no corrosion at terminals and proper fluid level). Cables securely fastened to battery.
- Condition of lanyard with one end securely connected to the lanyard stop switch.
- Attachment of safety chain, wire or line to boat and motor (applies to outboards fastened to the transom with screw clamps).

Outboard Starting Procedure

For best results, follow the procedures described in manufacturer's manual.
❶ Complete the inspection.
❷ Turn battery switch to correct setting.

This primer pump knob works differently from the traditional choke.

A *shear pin* breaks upon impact with the propeller, protecting the engine and the drive train from damage.

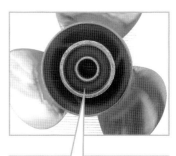

Most modern outboards use a *neoprene sleeve* bonded to the propeller hub that breaks upon impact with the propeller.

Retrieval line connecting motor and boat prevents motor from sinking to bottom if you lose your grip.

❸ Lower outboard into down position.

❹ Pump the fuel primer bulb until it is firm (if using a portable or integral tank, open its air vent before pumping the bulb). Also pump oil bulb, if applicable.

❺ Center outboard motor.

❻ Put gearshift in neutral and throttle to start position.

❼ If starting manually, activate the primer pump or pull the choke out all the way, then pull the starter cord until the engine starts. When using the cord remove any slack in it before pulling; don't yank on it or let it snap back on the rewind. On an outboard with a choke, once the engine fires, push choke in all the way (unless it is very cold). If after the third pull on the starter rope, the engine hasn't started, push the choke in halfway and pull the rope again.
If using an electric starter, activate primer pump by holding ignition key in while turning to ON position. It may be necessary to cycle the pump two or three times before engine fires. NOTE: *if starting a warm engine, do not use primer pump or choke.*

❽ Adjust throttle to steady idle.

❾ Check for a stream of water flowing from the inspection outlet for cooling water discharge. Important: If there is no water, turn off the outboard motor immediately to prevent damage from overheating.

❿ Check gauges, if applicable. NOTE: If engine won't start and there is a smell of gasoline, wait several minutes before attempting to start it again.

Lifting an outboard. A small outboard motor of 20 horsepower or less can usually be lifted and attached to a boat without too much effort. Although this is best done on land, when doing it on the water, tie the boat so it won't move around during the transfer. Have someone pass the outboard to a person in the boat. As a precaution against accidentally losing the motor overboard during the transfer, tie a retrieval line to the motor and fasten it to the dock or boat.

Outboard Cooling System

Most outboard motors are water cooled. The illustration tracks the flow of cooling water which enters through the cooling water intake, and is pushed up the water feed tube by a water pump and then circulates through waterways in the engine block. The water then flows back down the leg where it mixes with the exhaust gases and exits through the propeller hub. During its journey down the leg, a bit of the cooling water is diverted through the inspection outlet for cooling water discharge to let you know that the cooling system is working. Outboards smaller than five horsepower will usually have their exhaust outlet located just above the propeller instead of through the propeller hub.

Outboard Cooling System

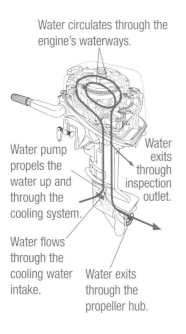

Water circulates through the engine's waterways.

Water pump propels the water up and through the cooling system.

Water exits through inspection outlet.

Water flows through the cooling water intake.

Water exits through the propeller hub.

Maintenance

Outboards should be kept in good operating condition by regular inspection and maintenance and serviced periodically by a qualified mechanic. A basic tool kit with spare parts for repairs and maintenance as well as manufacturer's manuals should be kept on board the boat in a waterproof container.

Basic Tools and Spares
- pliers
- spark plug wrench
- screwdrivers (various sizes and heads)
- knife
- sandpaper
- duct tape
- electrical tape
- spare shear pins (if applicable)
- cotter pins
- spare starter rope (if applicable)
- spare spark plugs

Outboard Fuel System

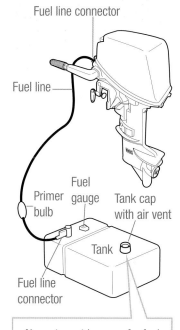

Fuel line connector

Fuel line

Fuel gauge

Primer bulb

Tank cap with air vent

Tank

Fuel line connector

Air vent must be open for fuel to flow to the outboard motor. It is usually closed when the boat is not being used.

REVIEW QUESTIONS

1. Two-stroke outboards are lubricated by oil that is _____ into the fuel while four-stroke engines are lubricated by oil in the _____.

2. When starting a cold outboard, either a primer pump is used to inject a small amount of _____ into the _____ or a choke is used to reduce the _____ supply in the _____.

3. When a propeller hits an object, the engine and drive train are protected from damage by the breaking of the bonding of the _____ to the propeller hub. On smaller outboards, the engine and drive train are protected by the breaking of a _____.

4. When starting an outboard, it is important to check for a stream of _____ from the inspection outlet. If there is no _____ , the outboard motor should be _____.

5. If starting a warm engine, do not use _____ or _____.

Answers: 1) mixed; crankcase 2) fuel; cylinder; air; carburetor 3) neoprene sleeve/hub; shear pin 4) water; water; turned off 5) primer pump; choke

3. Inboard Engine Systems

KEY CONCEPTS
- ▶ Types of engines
- ▶ Starting procedures
- ▶ Types of drives
- ▶ Maintenance

Inboard engines use either gasoline or diesel fuel. Gasoline engines with their relatively lighter weights and higher rpm often power high-performance sportboats. Diesel engines are typically used on large or moderate-speed vessels for their reliability and low-speed torque. Diesel fuel does not have the fire hazards of gasoline.

Gasoline Engine Systems

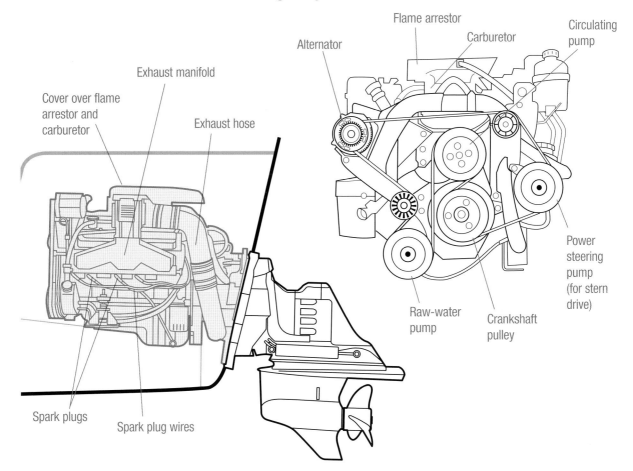

Gasoline Engine Inspection
- Oil level; add if indicated.
- Fuel tank level; add if indicated.
- Condition of fuel line (no cracks or sponginess) and connections.
- Any leaks in fuel system or gasoline odor in bilges.
- Belts should be snug; look for signs of wear.

- Raw-water seacock should be open.
- Raw-water strainer; clean out debris.
- Engine control levers operating smoothly.

Gasoline Starting Procedure. Follow procedures in the manufacturer's manual for recommended steps.

❶ Complete the inspection.
❷ Turn battery switch to correct setting.
❸ Engage engine blower and wait a couple of minutes.
❹ Tilt stern drive into down position and center it.
❺ Put gearshift in neutral and throttle slightly open.
❻ Turn ignition key to ON to start engine.
❼ Adjust throttle to steady idle.
❽ Check exhaust outlet for consistent water flow.
❾ Check gauges (oil pressure, water temperature, ammeter).

Diesel Engine Systems

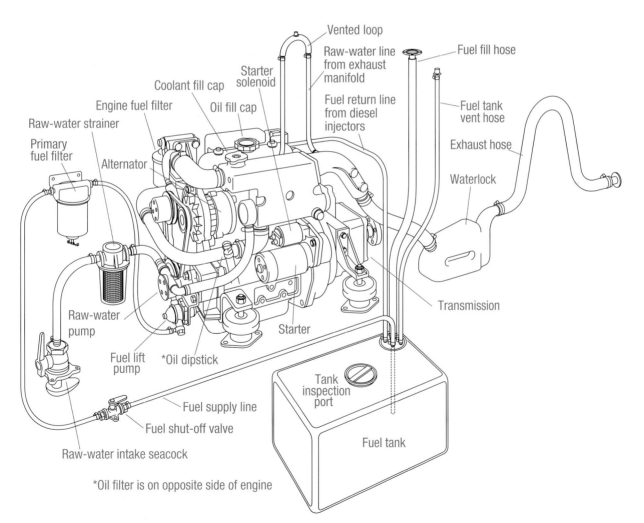

Diesel Engine Inspection
• Engine oil level; add if indicated.
• Coolant; add if indicated.
• Fuel tank level; add if indicated.
• Condition of fuel line (no cracks or sponginess) and connections.
• Belts should be snug; look for signs of wear.
• Engine pan and bilge for fuel, water or oil.
• Raw-water seacock is open.
• Raw-water strainer; clean out debris.
• Engine control levers for smooth operation.

Diesel Starting Procedure. Follow procedures in the manufacturer's manual for recommended steps.
❶ Complete the inspection.
❷ Turn battery switch to correct setting.
❸ Engage engine blower.
❹ Put engine stop control in RUN position.
❺ Put gearshift in neutral and throttle slightly open.
❻ Preheat with glow-plug control for 10-30 seconds, if applicable.
❼ Turn on ignition (oil pressure alarm should sound) and start engine.
❽ Adjust throttle to steady idle (oil pressure alarm should stop).
❾ Check exhaust outlet for consistent water flow.
❿ Check gauges (oil pressure, water temperature, ammeter).

A diesel engine is stopped by putting the engine stop control in the STOP position. After the engine stops, return the control to the RUN position and turn off the ignition key. CAUTION: *Do not stop engine when in forward or reverse gear.*

Cooling Systems

Nearly all inboard engines use seawater (raw-water) to cool the internal coolant, unlike a car which uses air to cool the internal coolant.

Types of Drives

Stern Drives. Stern drives, sometimes called inboard/outboards (I/O) or outdrives, combine features of both an inboard engine and outboard motor. The gasoline or diesel engine is mounted inside the boat and the power train goes through the transom to a stern drive that resembles the lower part of an outboard motor. The stern drive is turned to steer the boat and is also capable of being tilted upward when not in use.

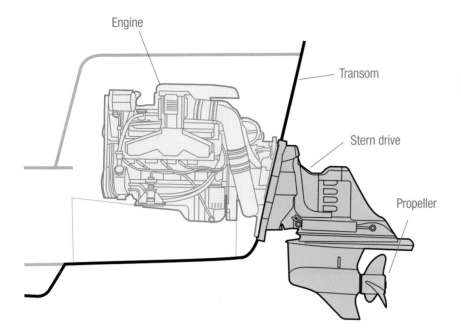

Shown is a typical stern drive driven by an inboard engine.

Stern Drive Inspection
• Hydraulic fluid for power trim control; add if indicated.
• Propeller blades and neoprene sleeve are intact.

"Fixed" (Non-Swiveling) Propeller Drives. The propeller shaft starts at the gearbox transmission and passes through a sealed stern tube in the bottom of the hull. Since the propeller cannot be turned like an outboard motor or stern drive, a rudder is required to steer the boat.

Shown is a typical fixed propeller drive driven by an inboard engine.

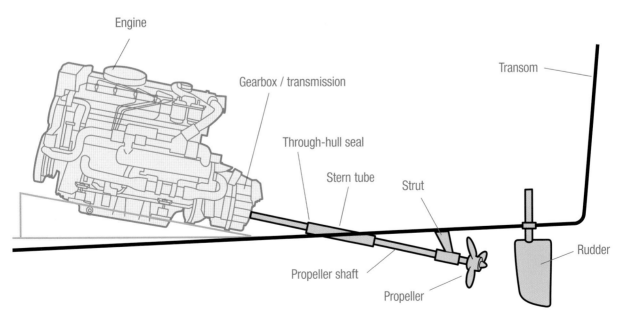

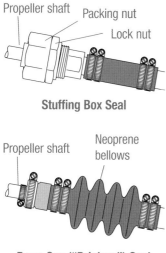

Stuffing Box Seal

Deep-Sea ("Dripless") Seal

Propeller shaft through-hull seal. There are various arrangements for keeping this joint watertight, one of which is the increasingly popular Deep-Sea seal. Another one is a stern gland where the shaft passes through a "stuffing box" on the inside of the hull. A packing nut on the stuffing box is tightened against the packing material to keep out the water.

Jet Drives. Jet drives use a large water pump impeller powered by either a gasoline or diesel engine to accelerate water flow through a nozzle to produce propulsive thrust. Jet drives have good steering ability at all speeds except when slowing down. Most mid- to large-size jet drives use deflectors for steering and reverse by deflecting the water flow from the nozzle to change direction. Smaller jet drives used on personal watercraft (PWC) and small sportboats may use a swiveling nozzle for steering and a reversing deflector.

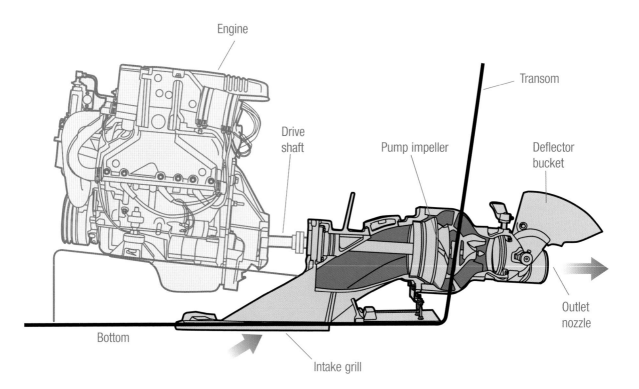

Jet Drive Inspection
• Jet drive control should operate smoothly.
• Hydraulic oil level; add if indicated.
• Condition of jet drive's impeller; inspect through access cover (engine must be turned off and transmission in neutral).
• Jet drive should rotate freely (engine must be turned off and transmission in neutral).

Bow and Stern Thrusters

Bow thrusters have become standard equipment on many large powerboats and are becoming increasingly popular on more moderate sized boats. Thrusters are used to increase a boat's maneuverability by moving either the bow (forward part) of the boat sideways with a bow thruster or the stern (after part) of the boat sideways with a stern thruster. Both types of thrusters typically use one or two propellers contained in a tunnel to generate sideways thrust. They are either electrically or hydraulically powered.

Maintenance

Consult the manufacturer's manual for recommended maintenance procedures. A basic tool kit with spare parts for repairs and maintenance as well as manufacturers' manuals should be kept on board the boat in a waterproof container.

Basic Tools and Spares
• pliers
• wrenches
• spark plug wrench (if applicable)
• screwdrivers (various sizes and heads)
• hammer
• knife
• sandpaper
• duct tape
• electrical tape
• spare spark plugs (if applicable)

Bow thrusters aid maneuverability in tight quarters by pushing the bow directly from side to side. Generally, they should only be used for short bursts.

REVIEW QUESTIONS

1. Inboard engines use either _____ or _____ fuel. _____ fuel does not have the fire hazards of _____.
2. When opened, a _____ fitting lets _____ in to cool the engine and exhaust gases.
3. After starting an inboard engine, it is important to check for _____ flowing out of the exhaust outlet. If there is no _____, immediately _____ the engine.
4. A diesel engine is stopped by
    a. turning the ignition key to the stop position
    b. turning the ignition key to the off position
    c. putting the stop control in the stop position
    d. engaging the stop brake on the propeller shaft
5. Jet drives have good steering ability at all speeds except when _____.

Answers: 1) gasoline; diesel; diesel; gasoline 2) seacock; water 3) water; water; turn off 4) c. putting the stop control in the stop position 5) slowing down

4. Preparation & Trip Planning

KEY CONCEPTS
▶ Preparation ▶ Trip planning

Preparation and planning are without question the most important ingredients in safe, enjoyable powerboating. Many of the things that can go wrong can be avoided with a bit of foresight.

Dress for Boating

Nothing takes the fun out of boating faster than being cold — or hot. Temperatures on the water tend to be more extreme and more changeable than ashore, so the right gear and clothing are an important part of enjoying your time on the water. Using the layered approach to clothing is the best way to stay comfortable in changing conditions. In cool weather, it's important to keep your head, hands and feet warm.

Because damaging ultraviolet (UV) rays can penetrate clouds and bounce off the water's surface, it's important to protect your eyes and skin. Apply sunscreen with a Sun Protection Factor (SPF) of 15 or higher that protects against both UVA and UVB rays. This will provide protection from both direct and reflected sunlight. Waterproof and "SPORT" sunscreens are available which will not run or rub into eyes. Wear sunglasses with good protection from:
• Sideways exposure
• UV rays (at least 90%)
• Glare off the water (polarized lenses)

Wearing life jackets (Personal Flotation Devices/PFDs) is comparable to wearing seat belts in a car. If you're wearing one, it could save your life in an emergency (such as falling overboard or your boat gets swamped with water). If your boat is registered anywhere in the U.S., your PFD must be U.S. Coast Guard approved. There are five types of approved PFDs; see Chapter 8 for more information on them. Your life jacket should be:
• an appropriate size
• fit properly so it doesn't ride up when you're in the water
• a visible color (yellow or orange are the most visible in the water)

A two-piece foul-weather gear set (waterproof jacket and pants, preferably with suspenders) is more versatile than a one-piece

Warm Weather Dressing

☐ Light-colored hat or visor with a dark color under the bill to reduce reflection.

☐ UV sunglasses with a keeper cord.

☐ Light-colored, lightweight cotton shirt. For sun-sensitive skin, a high collared shirt with sleeves helps protect neck and arms.

☐ Life jacket (PFD) in good condition zipped or clipped closed.

☐ Water-resistant watch.

☐ Long pants protects legs from prolonged exposure to the sun.

☐ Snug-fitting shoes with non-skid soles for firm traction on wet surfaces and foot protection.

☐ Soft, water-resistant duffel bag contains foul-weather gear, cold-weather or spare clothing, bathing suit, towel, sunscreen, and a water bottle.

Cold and Wet Weather Dressing

☐ A knit ski cap helps minimize heat loss through the head.

☐ Hood with brim and drawstring keeps head and neck dry and warm. A baseball cap worn under the hood provides the protection of a visor and keeps the hood out of your vision when turning your head.

☐ Fleece jacket with high collar with or without nylon shell. For colder conditions, add additional layers for warmth over synthetic (polypropylene, polyester) underwear.

☐ PFD worn outside foul-weather gear.

☐ Velcro or elastic cuffs at wrists and ankles help keep water out.

☐ Lined waterproof gloves keep hands dry and warm.

☐ Foul-weather gear offers protection from wind and water.

☐ For colder conditions, add a layer of fleece pants.

☐ Sea boots with wool or synthetic socks keep feet warm and dry.

PWC operators should wear a wetsuit or drysuit if air or water is cool

Two-piece foul-weather suits provide versatility in different temperatures and conditions.

jumpsuit. The jacket and pants can be worn together or separately to suit different temperatures and conditions. When selecting a size, make sure it is loose enough for layers of warm clothing underneath.

Checking Weather

Develop a habit of checking local conditions and forecasts before departure and be conscious of weather developments while underway. Be familiar with the prevailing weather patterns. The NOAA weather radio network broadcasts local and coastal marine forecasts on a continuous cycle. Most VHF radios can receive these broadcasts, usually on a channel listed as WX1, WX2, etc. There are numerous Internet websites, including the National Weather Service (NWS), that provide local marine weather information as well as weather chart analysis and forecasts, radar images, and warnings. If you know the web address of your local NWS office, you can save time by going there directly. Many television weather reports provide live radar coverage of your boating area. This is particularly valuable in determining the potential for thunderstorms. In any event, take time to get the best weather forecast available. (See Chapter 10 for more information about weather.)

ONLINE... National Weather Service local weather information: http://www.srh.noaa.gov/

Checking Tide and Current

When using a boat ramp or operating in tidal waters it is important to know the status of local tides to ensure there is enough water at the ramp or along your intended route. In many areas currents can have a major effect on navigation (particularly on slower boats) or using a ramp. Currents flowing perpendicular to the ramp in rivers and tidal estuaries can often make *launching* and *hauling out* a challenge. In these situations it is important to know the times of slack water (minimal or no current) and maximum current flow. Remember, slack water does not always coincide with high and low tide. Sources for tidal information include nautical almanacs, NOAA weather radio broadcasts, newspapers and television. Information concerning currents is a little more difficult to obtain, but is available from published tidal current tables for specific locations. (See Chapter 10 for more information about tides and currents.)

Local Hazards

It is also important to know of any special or out-of-the-ordinary situations that might affect you. These might include missing navigation marks, bridge closures, diving operations and dredging. A good source of this information is *Local Notices to Mariners*, which is published weekly by your local U.S. Coast Guard District and can be downloaded from the website of the U.S. Coast Guard Navigation Center. Local Notices are also generally available from marine stores, marinas, clubs or boating organizations. By addressing a request to your local Coast Guard District you may be placed on the Local Notices to Mariners mailing list. The U. S. Coast Guard also broadcasts Local Notices to Mariners information twice a day in its regular marine broadcast on Marine VHF Channel 22A. Special notices such as missing navigation marks are also broadcast as they occur in Safety Broadcasts on channel 16 in Urgent Marine Broadcasts.

ONLINE... *Local Notices to Mariners:* http://www.navcen.uscg.gov/lnm/

Take local weather hazards into account when planning a boating trip. These can include strong onshore sea breezes that occur as the land heats up during the day, squalls, thunderstorms, lightning and fog. (See Chapter 10 for more information.)

Navigation Plan

A Navigation Plan should be created in advance of your departure. Although every trip on familiar waters does not require a detailed navigation plan, there should be some method to find your way home. A laminated page showing compass headings from a conspicuous, lighted, sound-buoy (a navigation aid) to your destination can be invaluable in limited visibility. Unfamiliar waters demand a more detailed plan of compass headings, distances and estimated times that can be backed up with GPS positions of latitude and longitude.

Float Plan

Someone else should know your plan — where you plan to go, your route plan and departure and arrival times as well as a complete description of your boat, names of people on board, type of radio and boat name, and survival gear carried on board. Write this information down either on a sheet of paper or a prepared form. This is called a Float Plan. Give it to a friend or relative (not the Coast Guard) who can contact the Coast Guard if you don't return on schedule. Writing the information down is important. Not only is it difficult for someone to recall these details from memory, but the very process of writing it down forces you to think about your trip and plan more thoroughly. Upon your return, let your friend or relative know that you have arrived safely.

NAVLOG **RC TO FYC**

From	To	Crs	Dist	Speed	ETE	ETA	Remarks
RC	MK "E"	087	.5	5	0+06	0+06	
MK "E"	FG 7	048	2.3	6	0+23	0+29	
FG 7	FG 5	352	1.9	6	0+19	0+48	
FG 5	FYC	272	1.6	5.5	0+30	1+18	*Slow at 1+00*

This sample navigation plan depicts compass courses, distances, speeds and times for various marks along the route.

Sample Float Plan

Complete this form before going boating and leave it with a reliable person who can notify the Coast Guard or other rescue organization, should you not return as scheduled. Do not file this plan with the Coast Guard.

1. Person Reporting Overdue

Name _____ Phone _____

Address _____

2. Description of Boat

Registration/Documentation No. _____

Length _____ Make _____ Type _____

Hull Color _____ Trim Color _____ Fuel Capacity _____

Engine _____ No. of Engines _____

Distinguishing Features _____

3. Operator of Boat

Name _____ Age _____

Phone _____ Health _____

Address _____

Operator's Experience _____

4. Survival Equipment (Check as Appropriate)

No. of PFDs _____ No. of Flares _____ Mirror _____ Smoke Signals _____

Flashlight _____ Food _____ Paddles _____ Fresh Water _____

Anchor _____ Raft or Dinghy _____ EPIRB _____

Others _____

5. Marine Radio

☐ Yes, ☐ No Type _____ Freqs. _____

6. Trip Expectations

Depart from_____ Departure Date_____ Time_____

Going to_____ Arrival Date_____ Time_____

If operator has not arrived/returned by: Date _____ Time _____ call the Coast Guard or local authority at the following number: _____

7. Vehicle Description

License No. _____ Make _____ Model _____ Color _____

Where is vehicle parked?_____

8. Persons on Board

Name _____ Age _____ Phone _____

Medical Conditions _____

9. Remarks _____

_____

This sample Float Plan is similar to the one suggested by the U.S. Coast Guard's Office of Boating Safety.

Fueling

Procedure for 2-Stroke Outboards. Oil is mixed with the fuel to lubricate the engine. There are two different ways that this can be done. To determine which method applies to your outboard, check the owner's manual.

❶ *Adding oil to the fuel tank.* This method is most common in older engines. Oil is usually added first, followed by gasoline to help mix them. If the fuel tank is empty, put in a gallon of gasoline before adding the oil, then add the rest of the gasoline. Many outboards use a ratio of 1 pint of oil to 6 gallons of gasoline, but check the owner's manual for the proper ratio. Serious damage to the engine can be caused by using an improper mixture.

❷ *Adding oil to an oil tank.* Many newer 2-stroke outboards have oil tanks (either as part of the engine or separate) that automatically meter the oil into the gasoline according to the engine speed.

Procedure for 4-Stroke Outboards. These run on pure gasoline with the lubricating oil added separately to the crankcase.

Procedure for Diesel Engines. These run on diesel fuel with the lubricating oil added separately to the crankcase. Although diesel fuel is much less volatile than gasoline and is considered relatively risk-free when fueling, it is still a good practice to follow many of the safety precautions for gasoline fueling.

Make sure fuel is added only through the deck plate marked "fuel," "gas" or "diesel." Monitor the fuel flow continuously and wipe up any fuel spilled on deck.

Safety Precautions for Gasoline Fueling. When fueling always remember that gasoline vapor is heavier than air. It can gather in bilges or enclosed compartments and can be ignited by a spark.

• Tie boat to dock to prevent it from moving.
• Close all hatches and openings before fueling.
• Shut off engine and all electrical equipment.
• Don't smoke or use anything that might cause a spark (like matches, lighters or switches) during the fueling process.
• Passengers should be off boat.
• Make sure tank vents are open.
• Determine amount of fuel needed (do not use a metal dipstick that could cause a spark)
• Fill portable fuel tanks off the boat.
• When pumping gasoline into the fuel tank, keep the hose nozzle in contact with the tank or the fill pipe to prevent a buildup of static electricity that might cause a spark.
• Do not overfill or force gasoline through the air vents.
• Leave some space in the tank for thermal expansion of the fuel.
• After fueling, allow time for fuel to drain from the hose before removing nozzle from the tank.

- Close caps on fuel fills.
- Wipe up spillage immediately and deposit rag in open trashcan ashore. Follow up with a wash-down if spillage occurs on the boat.
- Open all hatches and openings and allow boat to ventilate for five minutes. Turn on blowers.
- Check for gasoline odor in bilges and compartments before starting.

Boarding

Your boat should be tied to the dock or slip to keep it from moving. Step aboard the boat where it's closest to the dock. If you're carrying something, place it in the boat first or have someone hand it to you after you're aboard. Use both hands to grab something solid on the boat. To get better balance when stepping onto a smaller boat, keep your body low by bending over or squatting. On small, light boats, try to step as closely as possible to the centerline to minimize tipping. Once you are in a boat, your weight may affect how the boat sits in the water. Position your weight so that the boat is level from side to side and neither the bow and stern are too far down.

Departure Checks

A simple laminated list can be an invaluable aid in assuring that nothing has been overlooked. Some of the items on your list should include:

- Prepare appropriate foods and liquids.
- Check current conditions and weather forecast.
- Determine tides and currents.
- Identify local hazards.
- Review relevant charts, updates and cruising guides.
- Prepare a Navigation Plan and estimate fuel requirements.
- Determine viable alternatives or ports of refuge.
- Prepare a Float Plan and leave it with someone.
- Check the required equipment is present, up to date and in good working order.
- Remove water that has accumulated in bottom of the boat.
- Add fuel for trip.
- Complete crew briefing.
- Complete the pre-start list.

Crew Briefing

Briefing people once they are on board the boat is an often overlooked, but very important safety measure. Too often, boat operators assume their crew have more experience than they actually have, and that they are competent swimmers with no medical problems (their health and swimming ability could become an issue, if they fall overboard or the boat swamps). The briefing should include the following:

- Identify crew's swimming ability and any relevant medical problems.
- Discuss the importance of keeping hands and feet inside the boat.
- Identify the "safe" (i.e., cockpit) and "danger" (i.e., side decks) areas on the boat.
- Point out location and discuss use of safety equipment, such as fire extinguishers, PFDs, bilge pumps, and flares.
- Indicate what is expected of crew when leaving or returning to the dock as well as while the boat is underway.
- Describe some simple emergency procedures, such as how to work the radio or turn off the engine.

When boarding smaller, lighter boats, step as closely as possible to the centerline to avoid tipping.

REVIEW QUESTIONS

1. With regard to clothing, the best way to stay comfortable in changing weather conditions is to use the _____ approach.
2. Local weather conditions and forecasts can be found on the Internet and television in addition to _____ marine weather reports on VHF radio.
3. The Local Notices to Mariners is a good source for information on _____.
   a. navigation plans
   b. ship departures
   c. clothing advice
   d. local hazards
4. A Float Plan should not be given to the Coast Guard, but to a _____ or _____.
5. After fueling, it is important to open all hatches and openings to allow the boat to ventilate because gasoline vapor is _____ than air and can gather in the bilges.

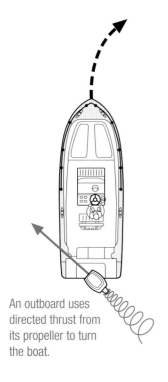

An outboard uses directed thrust from its propeller to turn the boat.

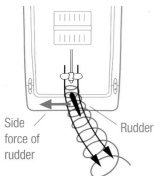

Side force of rudder | Rudder

A boat with a fixed propeller uses a rudder to turn the boat.

A rudder requires smooth water flow around it to function. Turning the rudder too sharply can stall flow and cause loss of steering.

5. Boathandling Concepts

KEY CONCEPTS

▶ Steering with directed thrust
▶ Steering with a rudder
▶ Prop walk
▶ Wheel & tiller steering

▶ Boat's pivot point
▶ Windage
▶ Minimum control speed
▶ Balance & trim

Steering with Directed Thrust

All boats with outboard motors, stern drives and jet drives use the *directed thrust* of the propeller or jet to steer the boat. To generate directed thrust, the propeller has to be turning (in forward or reverse gear) or the jet drive has to be pumping water through it. If the engine or jet drive is in neutral, the boat cannot be steered.

When the outboard motor is turned, the directed thrust from the propeller swings the stern (back end) of the boat, causing the boat to turn. To make a tighter turn, turn the outboard all the way to the side and increase the amount of thrust by increasing the throttle.

Steering with a Rudder

Boats with a "fixed" propeller drive use a rudder to produce a sideways force to turn the boat. Water must be flowing past the rudder to create this steering force. This flow is produced by the boat's motion through the water and by the propeller. As a boat moves faster, the steering ability of the rudder improves because the side force it generates increases as the speed of the water flow increases. To increase the effectiveness of a rudder in forward motion, it is normally placed behind the propeller to take advantage of the additional flow of water generated by the propeller (called *prop wash*). At very slow forward speeds you can use a burst of prop wash (by briefly increasing the throttle) to increase the flow of water passing the rudder, which increases the turning force. This is a technique often used when maneuvering at slow speeds in a confined area.

When a rudder is turned, it creates greater water pressure on one side than the other. This pressure difference generates lift as a sideways force that is used to turn the boat. For a rudder to work most effectively, the water must flow past it smoothly. If the rudder is turned too far or too quickly, water flow around it will "stall" and steering control will be lost or adversely affected.

Steering with Prop Walk (What is Prop Walk?)

Prop walk is a side force produced by the rotation of the propeller. This side force causes your boat to turn slightly rather than go in a straight line. Prop walk is most noticeable when the engine and propeller are operating in reverse on boats with a fixed propeller and rudder. A right-hand propeller in reverse "walks" the stern (back end) to port (left). A left-hand propeller will "walk" the stern to starboard (right). Increasing the throttle will increase the amount of prop walk, which will swing the stern even more.

This tendency can be put to good use if you anticipate which way it will move your boat. You can test your prop walk direction by putting the boat in reverse while still tied to the dock. Center the wheel and compare the amount of water flow (wash) on both sides of the boat. The stern will move away from the side with the greatest flow when in reverse.

Prop walk can be used to advantage in docking when the propeller is operating in reverse gear. You will want to approach the dock along the side of your boat that "walks" toward the dock. As you reach the dock, reverse your engine and let the stern "walk" right alongside.

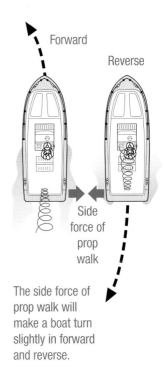

Forward

Reverse

Side force of prop walk

The side force of prop walk will make a boat turn slightly in forward and reverse.

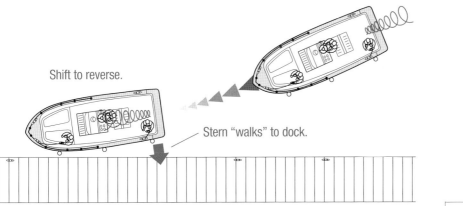

Shift to reverse.

Stern "walks" to dock.

Steering with a Bow Thruster

The directed thrust from the thruster's propeller is used to turn the bow (front end).

Steering with Twin Screws (Propellers)

A boat with twin screws can use thrust from an individual propeller or a combination of both for turning. When the port (left) propeller turns in forward gear and the starboard (right) propeller is in

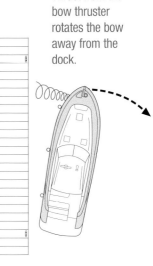

Thrust from the bow thruster rotates the bow away from the dock.

neutral, thrust will turn the boat to starboard (right) in a wide turn. To make an even tighter turn, put one propeller in forward gear and the other in reverse.

Using a Wheel to Steer

On boats equipped with wheel steering, turn the wheel in the direction you want to turn just as you would a car.

Using a Tiller to Steer

On boats equipped with tiller steering, move the tiller opposite to the direction you want to turn.

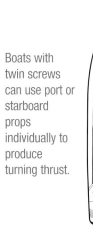

Boats with twin screws can use port or starboard props individually to produce turning thrust.

Using starboard prop only turns boat to port.

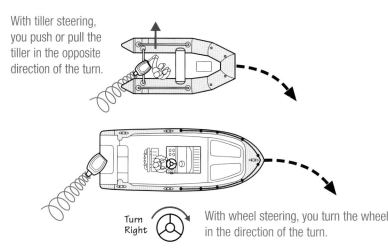

With tiller steering, you push or pull the tiller in the opposite direction of the turn.

Turn Right

With wheel steering, you turn the wheel in the direction of the turn.

Pivot Point

A boat's pivot point is the point around which it appears to turn. This point is normally located from 25% to 40% aft from the bow. As the boat starts to move forward, the pivot point shifts slightly forward and then moves aft as speed increases. When a boat turns, the relationship of the turning thrust at the stern to the pivot point causes the bow to rotate toward the direction of the turn and the stern to swing away from it.

When the boat goes backward, the pivot point appears to move aft considerably, causing the bow to swing in a wider arc than the stern.

Many good drivers imagine they are steering just the pivot point. They visualize the path they wish their pivot point to take over the water and then steer the point along that path. When a boat makes a turn, the first part of the turn will be wider than the rest of the turn.

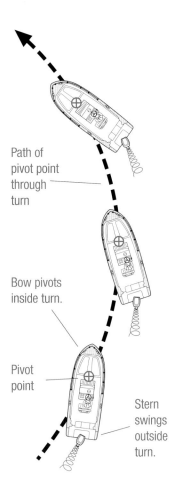

Path of pivot point through turn

Bow pivots inside turn.

Pivot point

Stern swings outside turn.

Windage

Wind will have an important effect on almost all of your boathandling maneuvers, especially when you operate at lower speeds in moderate to strong wind conditions. The wind's impact also varies with the amount of the boat's surface area (*windage*) that the wind can push against. Boats with high topsides, cabins and flying bridges have greater windage than boats with lower profiles.

When drifting, the wind will usually cause the bow to "fall off" until the boat lies across the wind or even with the stern toward the wind. This tendency to turn away from the wind is an important consideration when holding a boat in position.

When turning into the wind, windage reduces your speed and tightens your turning arc. This can be beneficial when maneuvering in a confined area.

When turning with the wind, windage increases your speed and enlarges your turning arc.

Underwater Hull Shape

A boat's underwater hull shape will affect its steering characteristics. Boats with minimal underwater profile, such as soft inflatables, will tend to skid or sideslip along the surface of the water as they turn, thereby increasing the turning arc. Turning this type of boat in windy conditions in a confined area is a true boathandling challenge.

Minimum Control Speed

Minimum control speed (mcs) is the slowest speed at which you can operate and still maintain steering control. Typically, this is less than the speed produced when the engine is in gear and the throttle is set at idle rpm, and is accomplished by the use of *intermittent power*. With the throttle at idle rpm, shift from neutral to forward and back to neutral. This produces a short, gentle pulse of power to maintain steering control. Repeat this technique to keep the boat under control and moving slowly. Minimum control speed is used in many situations such as docking and operating in confined areas. It is shown in the illustrations by ▶▶▶▶ (see page 45).

To make turns at minimum control speed, turn the wheel (*helm*) in the desired direction and shift into forward gear at idle rpm to start the turn, then back to neutral near the end of the turn. As a result of the directed thrust from the propeller (or increased water flow over

Wind Direction Clues
- *smoke from a smokestack*
- *flags onshore*
- *boats on moorings (usually point into the wind unless being affected by current)*
- *ripples or waves*
- *wind on your face (boat has to be stopped)*

Boats have a tendency to turn away from the wind.

WIND

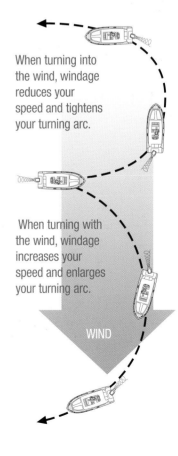

When turning into the wind, windage reduces your speed and tightens your turning arc.

When turning with the wind, windage increases your speed and enlarges your turning arc.

WIND

the turned rudder), the boat will turn but not accelerate significantly. When using intermittent power to turn, avoid oversteering and using too much throttle to prevent loss of steering control.

Balance and Trim

Boat balance and trim affect not only boat speed and fuel consumption, but also steering. A boat that does not have a level balance from side to side will want to turn. When making tight, high-speed turns, a boat out of balance could lose steering control and possibly capsize. You can correct balance by repositioning the weight of your passengers or gear and adjusting the trim tabs.

A boat with too much bow-down or bow-up trim will lose speed and is less responsive to steering. Too much bow-down trim may also bring the propeller too close to the water surface, causing it to ventilate and lose thrust. When this happens there will be a sudden increase in engine rpm and a sudden slowing in the boat.

Left side is lower.

This boat is not balanced from side to side and will turn.

Trim tabs are used to keep boat level and running straight.

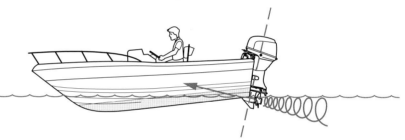

Outboard motor trimmed down produces bow-down trim.

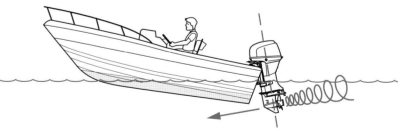

Outboard motor trimmed up produces bow-up trim.

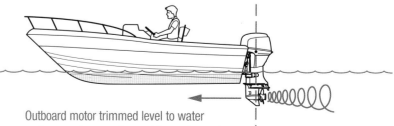

Outboard motor trimmed level to water surface produces optimum trim and speed.

A boat's fore and aft trim can be controlled by adjusting the up/down trim angle of the propeller or by adjusting trim tabs. A hydraulic trim control is used on larger outboards to adjust propeller angle. Smaller outboards can adjust it by moving a pin in the tilt control bracket.

Speed Modes

When a boat is moving, it will be operating in one of three speed ranges or speed modes:

Displacement Speeds. The boat rides through the water at almost level trim and is easy to steer and maneuver. As it approaches the semi-displacement mode, the stern squats and the bow rises as the boat's bow wave increases in size.

Semi-displacement Speeds. Most boats operate very inefficiently with high resistance at this speed. They have bow-high trim with the bow riding up the bow wave, producing maximum wave making (wake). They are sluggish to steer and maneuver. It requires a lot of power (throttle) to counteract the high resistance of the bow wave. In shallow waters, the stern will squat more, producing greater wake and the possibility of striking the bottom.

Planing Speeds. The boat rides on top of the water at close to level trim, supported by dynamic lift. Its wake has decreased in size, speed has increased significantly, and the boat responds quickly to small steering changes. Hydraulic trim controls can be adjusted to achieve optimum speed for a fixed throttle setting.

Changing Speeds

Increasing speed. The speed modes help to explain how a boat's operating characteristics change as power is added or reduced. As a boat increases speed, the bow raises and maintaining visibility becomes a problem, especially close ahead. Collision accidents are often the result of one or both boats operating in this mode of restricted visibility. Before opening the throttle, always check to make sure your course is clear of hazards. Whenever increasing speed raises the bow, either stand up (if the boat has a standup steering station or console) to maintain your close-ahead vision or do shallow S-turns.

Reducing speed. When slowing down from a planing speed to a displacement speed, the boat will transit through the semi-displacement range again, generating increased *wake* (waves).

In displacement mode, a boat glides smoothly in level trim with minimum wake.

In semi-displacement mode, the boat labors behind a large bow wave in bow-up trim. Maximum wake is produced.

In planing mode, boat rides level on top of water with less wake.

This is why a sudden stop from high speeds can result in wake breaking over the transom unless a high-speed stop maneuver is used (see page 41).

Boat Wake

Be considerate about the wake produced by your boat. Adjust your speed to reduce your wake when passing:
• boats tied to a dock or slip or rafted alongside each other
• boats in a mooring area or at anchor
• a sailboat with a person aloft on the mast

Reduce wake by operating at slower displacement speeds (preferably) or planing speeds. Operating at planing speeds in an anchorage is unsafe because of higher collision risk with another boat operating at high speed that may be hidden from view behind a moored boat. Changing speed to reduce wake should be made well in advance since it takes at least several boat lengths for your wake to settle down.

REVIEW QUESTIONS

1. With the engine in neutral, outboard motors, stern drives and jet drives have _____ steering.
   a. poor
   b. good
   c. excellent
2. The sideways force generated by a propeller is called _____.
3. As a boat increases speed its pivot point _____.
   a. moves forward
   b. remains the same
   c. moves aft
4. Steering a boat at minimum control speed requires _____ of power.
   a. no pulses
   b. gentle pulses
   c. strong pulses
5. A boat will produce maximum wake in the _____ mode.

Answers: 1) a. poor 2) prop walk 3) c. moves aft 4) b. gentle pulses 5) semi-displacement

6. Basic Boathandling

KEY CONCEPTS
- ▶ Leaving & returning
- ▶ Starting & stopping
- ▶ Holding position
- ▶ Turning maneuvers
- ▶ Securing a boat
- ▶ Knots & lines

An operator is responsible for the safety of the boat and everyone on board as well as others affected by his or her actions and attitude. A safe trip for all includes the following:

A responsible operator is always on the lookout for other vessels, hazards, swimmers and divers.

- Do not exceed the boat manufacturer's recommendations on the Maximum Capacities label. Exceeding either weight or horsepower limits can harm your boat's performance or even result in capsizing or swamping.
- Reduce the risk of falling overboard when underway by sitting in the seats, not on seatbacks, bow or side decks. Keep a secure grip on the boat, especially if you have to move around.
- Always maintain a good lookout for other vessels, hazards, and swimmers and divers.
- Always operate your boat at a safe speed and observe speed limits.
- Know how your boat performs and its limitations.
- Don't make sudden changes in speed and direction that can cause passengers to lose their balance or fall overboard. If you have to make a sudden change, give a timely warning.
- Monitor fuel to ensure you have enough to return with an adequate reserve.
- Follow your navigation plan and keep track of your position.
- Be alert for any weather changes and listen periodically for weather updates on the weather channel of your VHF radio.
- Know the Navigation Rules and use them to avoid collisions (see Chapter 11).
- Avoid impeding the passage of tug and barge traffic and large vessels that can only navigate within a channel.
- Be considerate of others using the water. Minimize the effect of your boat's wake. You are responsible for any damage caused by your wake.
- Be aware of the hazards of a propeller to people in the water. Position the boat to keep the propeller away from anyone in the water.
- Avoid disturbing the natural habitat of wildlife. In some areas, large animals share the waters, such as the manatee in Florida, which is particularly prone to being struck by boats.

Leaving a Dock

The following departure methods apply for most powerboats. In some cases they may need to be modified for rudder-steered boats with fixed propeller drives to compensate for, or take advantage of, the prop walk effect. Since the magnitude of the prop walk effect varies with different boats and propellers, you should know how your boat reacts to achieve proficient docking skills.

Key Points
* *Make sure everyone understands what to do with docklines and fenders.*
* *Check that no lines (ropes) are in the water before starting the engine.*
* *Start the engine using the manufacturer's recommended procedure.*
* *Stow docklines and fenders once clear of the dock.*

Back-Away Departure. Backing away from a dock usually offers the best maneuvering control. It also avoids a problem inherent to forward departures when the boat starts to turn and its stern (back end) swings into the dock, preventing the boat from departing cleanly.

Departure Using Directed Thrust Steering
❶ Turn wheel away from dock, which rotates propeller away from dock. If using a tiller, move it toward dock.
❷ Shift into reverse, stern (back end) swings away from dock as boat backs away. To avoid scraping the bow (front end) against dock, keep your turn small until bow clears dock.
❸ When clear of dock, turn wheel or tiller in opposite direction to turn boat parallel to dock.
❹ Center wheel or tiller, pause briefly in neutral while counting 1-2-3, then shift into forward.

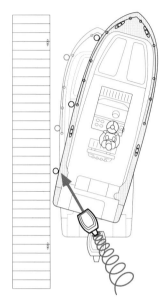

During a forward departure from a dock, the stern can swing into the dock, preventing the boat from completing its turn.

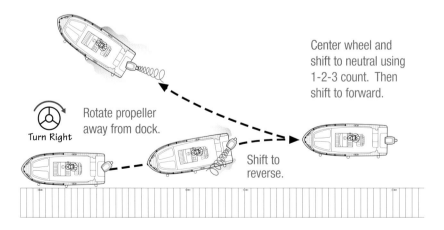

Center wheel and shift to neutral using 1-2-3 count. Then shift to forward.

Turn Right

Rotate propeller away from dock.

Shift to reverse.

Departure Using Rudder Steering and Prop Walk. For boats where prop walk will swing the stern (back end) toward the dock in reverse gear, you will have to use the rudder to counteract prop walk. As the boat gains backward speed, the rudder will become more effective allowing you to reduce rudder angle. If the prop walk force is too strong to overcome with the rudder, you will have to use a spring line (see Chapter 7).

For boats where prop walk will swing the stern away from the dock in reverse, you can usually center the wheel and rudder and let prop walk do the turning.

❶ Turn wheel and rudder away from dock.
❷ Shift into reverse, rudder side force overcomes prop walk, and stern swings away from dock.
❸ Center wheel and rudder, and shift into forward after pausing briefly in neutral while counting from 1 to 3 (the 1-2-3 count).

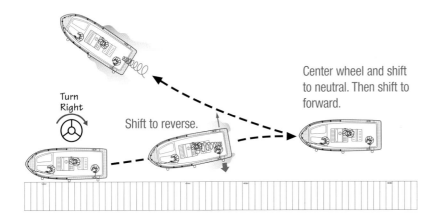

Center wheel and shift to neutral. Then shift to forward.

Turn Right

Shift to reverse.

Straight-Ahead Departure. This method is often used when a boat is positioned near the end of a dock and can clear the dock with little, if any, turning. It can also be used if a crosswind or crosscurrent will make the boat drift clear of the dock. Remember that when turning, your stern (back end) will swing outside your intended track and could hit the dock.

❶ Center outboard (or rudder), release docklines.
❷ Shift into forward gear and steer a straight course until clear of dock.
❸ Turn when clear of dock.

CAUTION: *An injury could occur when using a hand or foot to push a boat away from a dock. If you have to push off, sit or stand in the cockpit and use a boat hook (pole).*

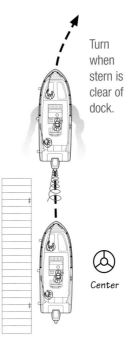

Turn when stern is clear of dock.

Center

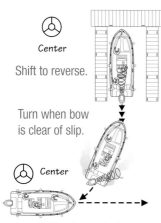

Center

Shift to reverse.

Turn when bow
is clear of slip.

Center

Shift to forward after
1-2-3 count in neutral.

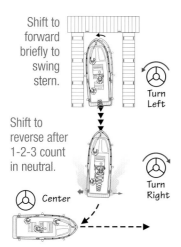

Shift to
forward
briefly to
swing
stern.

Turn
Left

Shift to
reverse after
1-2-3 count
in neutral.

Turn
Right

Center

Shift to forward after
1-2-3 count in neutral.

Steady your throttle hand against
the base in conditions where wake
or waves are present.

Leaving a Slip

Departure Using Directed Thrust Steering
❶ Center wheel (or tiller) and shift into reverse, slowly backing straight out.
❷ Turn boat once bow is clear of slip.
❸ Center wheel (or tiller) and shift into forward after pausing in neutral for the 1-2-3 count.

Departure Using Rudder Steering and Prop Walk.
With many boats, you can counteract the effect of prop walk by using the rudder to back straight out of the slip. Once your bow clears the slip, the rest of the steps are similar to those described for boats with directed thrust steering (see above). However, if the prop walk effect is so strong that the stern swings into the dock even with the rudder turned against it, you will have to get someone on the slip to move the boat far enough out of the slip so the stern and the bow clears it or use the pivoting maneuver described below. Another alternative is to use a spring line to pivot the boat, which is covered in Chapter 7.

❶ Turn wheel and rudder toward dock and briefly shift into forward, just enough to swing stern away from dock (in opposite direction of prop walk) without moving forward.
❷ Shift into neutral and allow pivoting momentum to continue until boat has pivoted enough to offset prop walk.
❸ Turn wheel and rudder away from dock and shift into reverse, slowly backing out. If boat swings too close to dock, shift into neutral and repeat steps 1, 2 and 3.

Starting

Putting a boat in motion involves shifting into forward or reverse gear at a low throttle setting and then adjusting the throttle to achieve the desired speed. *The key concept to remember when shifting to forward, neutral or reverse is that it should be done at idle rpm* to prevent damage to the engine or transmission.

Using the Throttle Control. Changes in the throttle control should be done in a smooth gradual manner. When operating in conditions where the boat could impact waves or wakes, steady your hand on the base of the control and adjust the throttle with thumb and fingers.

Stopping

When stopping or slowing down rapidly, steering control will initially be reduced because the boat's speed is not slowing as quickly as thrust is being reduced. In fact, if a boat traveling at high speed has its power cut suddenly, you may lose steering control completely. Whenever possible, put your boat on a straight course before slowing down and stopping.

Coasting Stop. To stop, reduce the throttle gradually, then shift into neutral. You can stop without using reverse, but you need to allow distance for coasting to a stop. Less coasting distance is needed if you stop heading into the wind. Larger and heavier boats carry more momentum and coast farther than small boats. The larger the boat, the more distance it will coast.

Quick Stop. If a boat needs to be stopped more quickly in a shorter distance:
❶ Gradually reduce throttle to idle rpm.
❷ Shift into neutral and pause while you count 1-2-3.
❸ Shift into reverse and increase throttle slightly to overcome forward momentum and stop boat.
❹ Immediately bring throttle to idle rpm and shift into neutral.

High-Speed Stop. While it's recommended to gradually reduce boat speed before stopping, you may be faced with a situation where you need to stop quickly at higher speeds. In addition to the possibility of momentarily losing steering control, there is a risk in some boats of the boat's wake coming over the transom and filling up the well or cockpit. To avoid this flooding problem, use the following maneuver:
❶ Reduce throttle to idle rpm.
❷ Make a 90-degree turn.
❸ Shift into neutral.

Holding Position

There are times when you may have to hold your boat in a specific location such as helping a boat in trouble, waiting for a bridge to open or waiting for room at a dock. The key to holding position is to anticipate boat drift and make small, gentle corrections early rather than large powerful corrections late.

Holding Bow into Wind. Since the bow will usually have a tendency to turn away from the wind, you will have to compensate for this by periodically shifting into forward gear and making slight steering corrections to bring the bow back into the wind. Don't let the bow fall off (turn away from the wind) too much. When the bow is pointed into the wind, shift back to neutral and drift back to your holding position. If the boat drifts downwind of the position, shift into forward gear to bring it back in position. Repetitive small adjustments must be

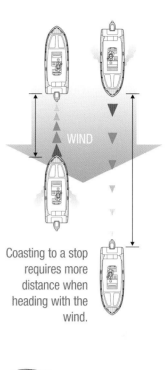

Coasting to a stop requires more distance when heading with the wind.

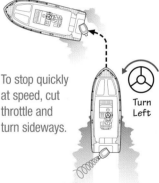

To stop quickly at speed, cut throttle and turn sideways.

Turn Left

WIND

Turn prop small amount and shift to forward to bring bow back into wind.

Turn Right

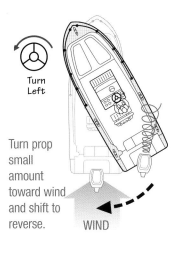

Turn prop small amount toward wind and shift to reverse.

WIND

Turn Left

made to maintain a holding position, especially as the wind increases. When current has more influence than wind, hold position with the bow or stern into the current, not the wind.

Holding Stern into Wind. Because the bow wants to turn downwind, it is usually easier to hold position with the stern into the wind, provided waves don't come over the transom (back end). Shift into reverse to keep the stern headed into the wind and to compensate for drifting. In windy conditions, you may have to switch to holding the bow into the wind to avoid exposure to exhaust gases or taking water over the back of the boat.

Turning Maneuvers

When making a turn, a key concept to remember is that a boat rotates around a pivot point, which causes the stern to swing out wide of your turning path. Keep this in mind when passing close to an object in the water. While your boat's bow and pivot point may clear the object, your stern could hit it. Remember, the pivot point for every boat differs and is influenced by a boat's windage and underwater shape.

Low-Speed Turn. At low speeds, the thrust from a propeller or jet is reduced in proportion to the effects of windage, causing some loss of turning maneuverability. In tight maneuvering situations in marinas or windy conditions, it may be necessary to use pulses of increased thrust by intermittently increasing the throttle a bit to improve turning control or achieve tighter turns.

Pivot Turn Using Directed Thrust. This is a maneuver frequently used in marinas or other very confined spaces to rotate a boat within a space of one to two boat lengths.
❶ Starting at rest, turn wheel hard over and shift into forward gear at idle rpm to initiate pivot turn.
❷ Shift into neutral and turn wheel hard over in opposite direction, while counting 1-2-3.
❸ Shift into reverse at idle rpm to continue turn.
❹ Shift into neutral and turn wheel hard over in opposite direction, while counting 1-2-3.
❺ Repeat until boat has completed its turn.
NOTE: To rotate the boat in the opposite direction, just reverse the direction of the wheel listed in steps 1, 2 and 4.

Pivot Turn Using Rudder Steering and Prop Walk. Use prop walk and water flow (prop wash) over the rudder to help turn the boat. Remember, water must be flowing past the rudder for it to have any effect. It is important to know the direction of the side force

Pivot Turn

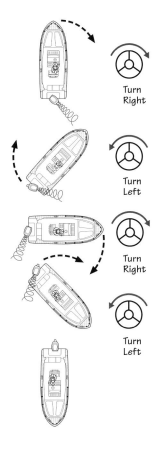

Turn Right

Turn Left

Turn Right

Turn Left

(prop walk) generated by the rotation of the propeller in reverse. If your boat "walks" its stern to port (left) in reverse, then you should rotate the boat clockwise by following these steps:

Pivot Turn

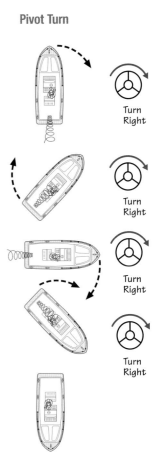

❶ Starting at rest, turn wheel hard over to starboard (right) and shift into forward gear, adding a small, gentle amount of throttle to generate water flow over rudder to initiate turn.

❷ Before gaining headway, shift into reverse (after pausing in neutral for the 1-2-3 count) and prop walk will swing stern to port. Keep wheel hard over to starboard throughout turn.

❸ Shift into forward gear (after pausing in neutral for the 1-2-3 count).

❹ Shift into reverse (after pausing in neutral for the 1-2-3- count) and use prop walk again.

❺ Repeat until boat has completed its turn.

If your boat kicks its stern to starboard in reverse, then rotate the boat counterclockwise by reversing the direction of the wheel in step 1.

Sharp Turn. (*Executing this maneuver at high speeds can be dangerous and is not recommended.*) Prior to executing a sharp turn, look around to make sure it is safe to turn and alert your passengers to hold on for the turn. Once this has been done, turn the wheel hard over and advance the throttle. When making a sharp turn most small powerboats will roll or heel significantly.

If the turn is executed at too high a speed, air may be drawn into the propeller, resulting in loss of thrust and a sudden increase in engine rpm. If this happens, reduce the throttle and the turn.

Avoidance Turn. This maneuver is used to prevent the stern of your boat from swinging into an obstacle when you've turned too late or too close. As soon as the bow is abreast of the obstacle, you should quickly reverse the turn to swing the stern back away from the obstacle.

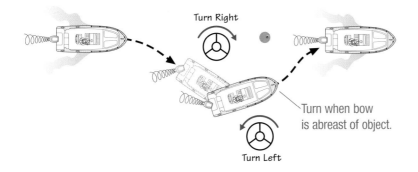

Turn Right

Turn when bow is abreast of object.

Turn Left

High-Speed Turn. Prior to making a high-speed turn, check to see that it is clear and safe to turn, and alert your passengers. Turn the wheel gradually and deliberately to maintain control throughout the

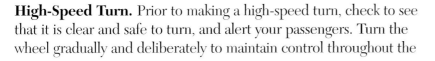

WIND

When backing a boat, use small steering adjustments to keep it under control.

WIND

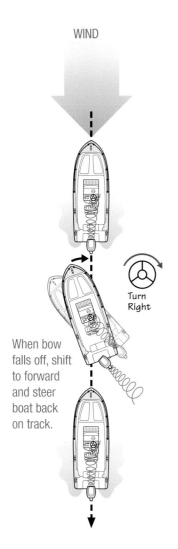

Turn Right

When bow falls off, shift to forward and steer boat back on track.

maneuver. The greater the speed, the wider and more gradual the turn should be. If the turn is too sharp, the propeller will ventilate and turning control will be lost.

Driving Backward

Key Points
• Wind direction: the bow will tend to turn downwind.
• Sea conditions: backing smaller outboard boats into waves may result in water coming over the transom and flooding the well or cockpit. If this starts to happen, abandon this maneuver.
• The pivot point will move aft in reverse, and depending on the boat's underwater shape and windage, it may move essentially to the propeller. This is particularly true for outboards or stern drives.
• Steering control: when backing and turning in reverse, use small steering adjustments. Too large or too fast adjustments can lead to a loss of control.
• Prop walk: on boats that are steered with a rudder, you will have to use the rudder to counteract the turning tendency of prop walk. On some boats, prop walk may be too strong for the rudders to overcome.

Backing Toward the Wind. The combination of windage and pivot point will help you hold your course.

Backing Downwind. It may be more difficult to maintain your course when backing downwind. If the bow falls off too much, you will lose steering control. Before this happens, shift to forward gear and bring the boat back on course. Then back up again with perhaps a slight steering correction to compensate for the wind's effect.

Returning to a Dock

To master this important maneuver you need to be aware of how your powerboat steers and reacts to changes of throttle and gearshift in different wind and current conditions. Here, your ability to maneuver at minimum control speed (mcs) will play an important role. A common mistake, especially with boats that use directed thrust steering, is to oversteer at slow speeds, which result in loss of control of direction. It is far better to use small steering adjustments at minimum control speed with only an occasional brief, small increase in throttle to make a sharper turn. The critical time for a safe and successful docking usually starts as you make your final turn to come alongside the dock and ends as you reverse to stop the boat. Here, you'll need precise adjustment and coordination of throttle, gearshift and wheel (or tiller).

Key Points
- *Place fenders at dock level and prepare docklines before making the final approach.*
- *Be sure everyone knows in advance what to do with the docklines.*
- *Whenever possible, come alongside the dock with the bow pointing into the wind or current, whichever is stronger.*
- *Make your approach at minimum control speed, which will avoid or minimize damage should reverse suddenly not be available.*
- *In the absence of wind or current, boats with rudder steering should approach the dock in a direction where prop walk will swing the stern toward the dock in reverse.*

Docking Tips. *Minimum control speed allows you to make a smooth easy turn. Faster approach speeds require a more abrupt turn and timing becomes more critical. Always have an escape plan in case you misjudge your approach.*

Small-Angle Approach. This is the easiest approach to use because it requires only small adjustments of steering and power controls. It also accommodates temporary changes in wind conditions (unlike an approach parallel to the dock, which requires more precision and is less tolerant of changing conditions).

❶ Approach dock slowly at a 20 - 25 degree angle. If approach speed is too fast, shift into neutral to slow boat and use intermittent power to maintain minimum control speed (mcs).

❷ When bow is about ½ to 1 boat length away from dock, make a smooth turn to bring boat parallel and close to dock. As bow starts to turn, shift into neutral.

❸ Reverse to stop boat.

❹ Shift to neutral. After boat is tied to dock, turn off engine.

Small-Angle Approach with Prop Walk.

❶ Approach dock slowly at a 20 - 25° angle on side where prop walk will pull your stern toward dock.

❷ When bow is about ½ to 1 boat length from dock, shift into neutral and make a smooth turn to bring boat close to dock and almost parallel.

❸ When bow is close to the dock, center rudder (wheel) and shift into reverse to stop. Prop walk will swing stern into dock. If stern needs to be brought in more or faster, turn rudder (wheel) toward dock and gently increase throttle.

Large-Angle Approach. In a situation where the wind pushes the boat away from the dock during its approach, you should increase your approach angle to head more into the wind. This increased angle will result in a tighter turn, which will increase the momentum of the swinging stern. If the stern swings too fast, you can prevent it from

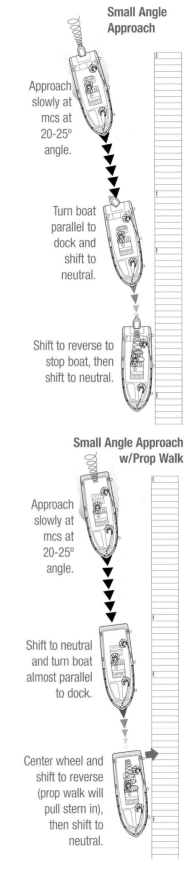

Small Angle Approach

Approach slowly at mcs at 20-25° angle.

Turn boat parallel to dock and shift to neutral.

Shift to reverse to stop boat, then shift to neutral.

Small Angle Approach w/Prop Walk

Approach slowly at mcs at 20-25° angle.

Shift to neutral and turn boat almost parallel to dock.

Center wheel and shift to reverse (prop walk will pull stern in), then shift to neutral.

Large Angle Approach

Approach slowly at mcs at 45° angle.

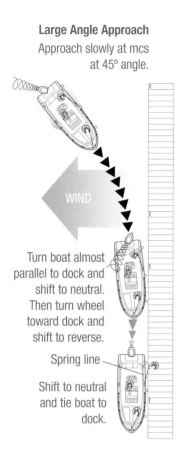

Turn boat almost parallel to dock and shift to neutral. Then turn wheel toward dock and shift to reverse.

Spring line

Shift to neutral and tie boat to dock.

hitting the dock with a small turn of the wheel away from the dock as you reverse to stop the boat. As you come alongside, the wind will try to blow the boat away from the dock, so it is important to stop quickly and pass a *line* (rope) to the dock without delay. The best line to use is one that is fastened to the boat halfway between the bow and stern (*amidships*) and led aft to a dock cleat. If the boat starts to drift away before the other docklines are tied, you can put the boat in forward gear at idle rpm and the spring line will bring the boat alongside the dock again and hold it there.

As the velocity of the wind increases, the power required to maintain minimum control speed (mcs) will have to be increased to overcome the increased drag from windage, which reduces the forward speed of the boat.

❶ Approach dock at approximately 45° angle at a minimum control speed that maintains steering control against the wind.

❷ When bow is close to dock, turn boat almost parallel to dock, but maintain a small angle to compensate for the wind's tendency to push bow downwind.

❸ When bow is a couple of feet from dock, shift into neutral, pausing briefly for the 1-2-3 count, and then shift to reverse, turning wheel toward dock and using a small amount of throttle to bring stern in as the boat stops.

❹ As soon as boat is alongside, shift into neutral and quickly tie aft spring line in case it's needed to hold boat to dock. After other docklines are tied, turn off engine.

Returning to a Slip

Upwind Approach. In this situation you can use the wind to help slow the boat as you bring it into the slip. Have docklines ready to help stop the boat moving forward or backward too much in the slip.

❶ Approach at minimum control speed (mcs) and make a wide turn to line up boat to slip.

❷ As bow starts to enter slip, shift into neutral to slow boat.

❸ Reverse to stop boat, then shift to neutral and secure docklines.

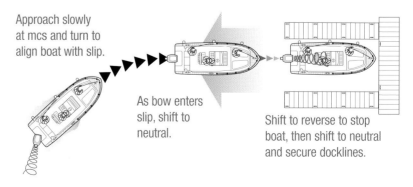

Approach slowly at mcs and turn to align boat with slip.

As bow enters slip, shift to neutral.

Shift to reverse to stop boat, then shift to neutral and secure docklines.

Securing a Boat

A powerboat can be tied alongside a dock with two spring lines and single bow and stern lines or it can be positioned in the middle of a slip with two bow lines and two stern lines.

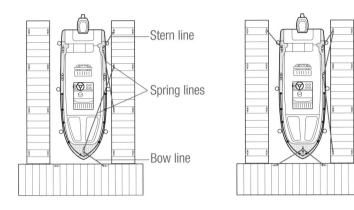

Stern line

Spring lines

Bow line

Boathandling Basics for Personal Watercraft

- *Read the operating instructions and familiarize yourself with stop/start and throttle controls. Take into consideration many PWCs have no neutral or reverse.*
- *Be aware that steering control is drastically reduced or lost when going rapidly from high to low speed (the PWC is moving faster through the water than the steering thrust of the jet drive).*
- *Keep a constant lookout for other boats and objects.*
- *Always look around before turning.*
- *Be considerate of other boaters and people onshore — avoid operating in the same area for any length of time and avoid making excessive noise (altered mufflers or cutout devices are prohibited in many states).*
- *Know how to get back on your PWC.*
- *Do not make sudden changes in direction when near other boats.*
- *Do not reverse at high speeds, if PWC is equipped with a reverse.*
- *Do not wake jump close behind another boat (many states prohibit this within 100 feet).*
- *Do not disable the self-circling device, if PWC is equipped (req).*

Knots

Safe powerboating requires basic seamanship functions such as tying up to a dock, using fenders, securing an anchor line, taking a tow and giving another boat a tow. All of these cases involve handling a line (rope) and tying a secure knot that is also easy to untie.

Cleat Hitch. A cleat hitch is used to tie a line to a cleat. If tied properly, the line won't jam or slip on the cleat.

Cleat Hitch

Lead the line around the far end of the cleat and wrap it around the base.

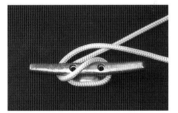

Cross the line over the top and around the horn.

Then twist the line to form a loop around the other horn.

The end of the line should parallel the part of the line that was originally crossed over the top of the cleat.

Round Turn with Two Half-hitches. This knot can be used to secure fender lines to rails or stanchions.

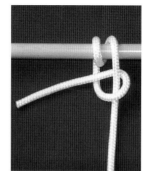 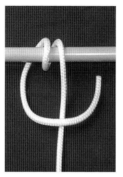 

Wrap the end of the line *twice* around the object.

Cross the end over and around the standing part, passing it inside to form a half-hitch.

Again, cross the end over and around the standing part, passing it inside to form a second half-hitch.

Sheet Bend

Make a loop at the end of the larger line, with the bitter end crossing over on top. Run the smaller line up through the loop.

Run the smaller line down around the standing part of the larger line, up over the edge of the loop, and down through the loop again.

Tighten the knot.

Bowline. This knot can be used to make a non-slipping loop at the end of a line to put over a piling or cleat. It becomes more secure under pressure, but remains easy to untie when pressure is released. In situations where the load on the line is not constant, it can work loose. For that reason, it is not recommended for tying an anchor line to an anchor.

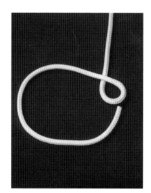  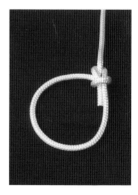

Put a small loop in the line where you want the knot to be, for example, about 18 inches from the end. Make sure the end crosses on top of the standing part of the line. This small loop will end up as part of the knot.

Pass the end up through the loop you just made, down behind the standing part, back up over the edge of the loop, and down through the loop again.

Tighten the knot, making sure the knot holds and the remaining loop does not slip.

Sheet Bend. A sheet bend is used to tie two different size lines together.

Handling Docklines with End Loops

Normal practice when approaching a dock is to give the person on the dock the end of the line with the loop in it and then direct him where to place the line. The line is then adjusted from the boat.

Using a Loop on a Cleat. If a loop is simply slipped over a cleat, changes in tension and angle of the line could cause the loop to jump off the cleat. Taking a turn around the cleat with the loop reduces this possibility. Another method is to pass the loop through the opening of the cleat before putting it over the ends (horns) of the cleat. A loop on a cleat cannot be freed if it is under load.

Dipping a Loop

The loop of the larger line has been dipped under and inside the smaller line's loop before passing it over the piling.

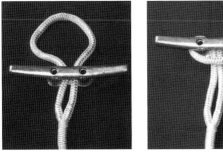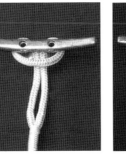

Pass the loop through the opening in the cleat. Then pass the end of the loop over the horns and tighten the line.

Taking a turn around a cleat with the loop reduces the possibility of the loop jumping off accidentally.

Dipping a Loop. If a line is to be placed around the piling and another boater has his loop already around the piling, your loop should be passed up through the other boat's loop before being placed over the top of the piling. This allows either boat to leave without removing the other loop.

Making a Larger Loop. If the loop on a line is too small to fit around the piling, the line can be passed through the loop to make a larger one.

Types of Line

There are several different types of line (rope) used on boats:

- Nylon is commonly used for anchor lines (rodes) and docklines because of its strength and ability to stretch, which helps absorb shock loads.
- Polyester or Dacron line has less stretch and less ultimate strength than nylon, but is easy on the hands. It is a good all-purpose line.

Making a Larger Loop

Grab the line about 18 inches below the loop and pass it through the loop.

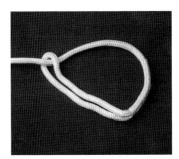

Then pull on the line. The part of the line closest to the loop will pass completely through, forming a larger loop.

• Polypropylene line is not as strong as Nylon or polyester line and is very sensitive to UV radiation, but it floats, which makes it popular for waterskiing towlines. It has a slippery surface and doesn't bend easily, so be careful when tying knots in polypropylene line.

Coiling a Line

When you have finished using a line, it should not be simply left in a tangled pile. Idle lines should always be coiled so they are ready to use or release.

When coiling a line, one hand makes a new loop that is fed onto the other hand holding the loops previously coiled. Twisted (i.e., three-strand) lines are sensitive to whether they are coiled in a clockwise or counterclockwise direction. This is a function of the direction the fibers are twisted when they are made. Most twisted lines are twisted in a right-handed direction and should be coiled in a clockwise direction, otherwise they will kink when uncoiling. For braided lines, where fibers are not twisted, loops may need to be alternated in direction or coiled in figure-8s.

Stowing a Coiled Line. To prepare a coiled line for stowing, wrap the end of the line around the middle of the coil. Make a loop and pass it through the upper hole in the coil and over the top of the coil. Then pull the end of the line to tighten and secure the loop.

Heaving a Line

When preparing to throw a line, first make sure one end is secured on your boat. Hold half of the coil in your throwing hand and the other half in your other hand. Swing and throw the coil underhand, allowing the remainder of the line to run free from your other hand. Don't throw the line right at the person, but just to the side.

With some lines, it helps to twist the line slightly as it is coiled.

When stowing coiled lines, secure the coil with a loop.

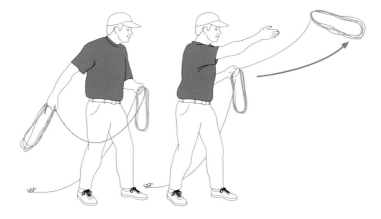

REVIEW QUESTIONS

1. To avoid having the stern of your boat swing into the dock, the recommended departure method is to _____ from the dock.
2. When shifting gears from forward to reverse, it is possible to damage the engine or transmission unless the gears are shifted at _____ rpm.
3. To avoid the boat's wake from coming in over the transom when making a high-speed stop, you should reduce the throttle to idle rpm, make a _____ turn and shift into _____.
4. A type of turn frequently used in marinas and other confined spaces that turns a boat within a space of 1 to 2 boat lengths is called a _____.
5. Due to its ability to stretch more than other types of line, the type of line generally preferred for anchor and docking lines is _____.
   a. Dacron
   b. nylon
   c. polypropylene

Answers: 1) back away 2) idle 3) 90-degree: neutral 4) pivot turn 5) b. nylon

7. Advanced Boathandling

KEY CONCEPTS
▶ Anchoring
▶ Spring line departures
▶ Returning to dock & slip
▶ Coming alongside a boat
▶ Locks
▶ High-speed maneuvers
▶ Heavy weather maneuvers
▶ Twin-screw maneuvers

Advanced boathandling builds on the fundamental skills introduced in the previous chapter and enables you to deal with more challenging boating situations.

Anchoring

For a variety of reasons there will be times when you will anchor your boat. Following are some procedures for setting and retrieving an anchor as well as information to help you select a suitable anchoring location.

Anchoring Tips
• *Check the water depth on a chart. If there is tide, make sure there is enough depth at low tide and enough rode (anchor line and chain) at high tide.*
• *Make sure there are no obstructions above or below the water that your boat could hit when it swings on its anchor.*
• *Try to anchor in calmer protected waters by choosing a location in the lee (downwind) of land or a breakwater.*

Your boat will rotate on its anchor with wind and current changes, so make sure your swing circle will keep you clear of all obstructions.

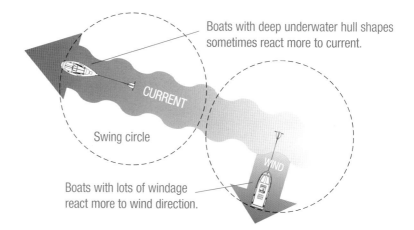

Boats with deep underwater hull shapes sometimes react more to current.

CURRENT

Swing circle

WIND

Boats with lots of windage react more to wind direction.

• *Check your chart to avoid grassy bottoms which are difficult for setting lightweight anchors.*
• *Do not anchor in channels, high traffic areas or near underwater cables.*
• *Take a pass around the intended anchoring area to check for any uncharted hazards.*

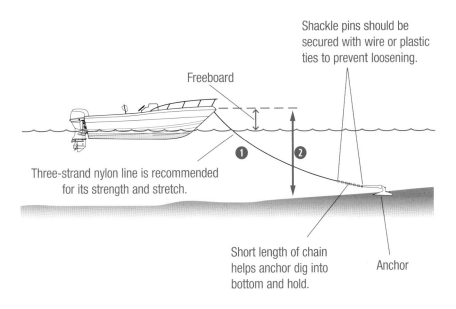

Shackle pins should be secured with wire or plastic ties to prevent loosening.

Freeboard

Three-strand nylon line is recommended for its strength and stretch.

Short length of chain helps anchor dig into bottom and hold.

Anchor

Example:
If water depth plus freeboard ❷ = 7 feet and if you let out 35 feet of rode ❶,

$$\text{Scope} = \frac{35 \text{ feet}}{7 \text{ feet}} = \frac{5}{1} \quad \text{or } 5{:}1$$

If the tide rises 3 feet, scope $= \dfrac{35 \text{ feet}}{10 \text{ feet}} = \dfrac{3.5}{1} \quad$ or 3.5:1

and your anchor may drag unless you let out more line.

How well an anchor holds is determined by three primary factors:
• anchor type and size
• bottom type (i.e., mud, sand, clay), and
• the amount of scope, which is the ratio of length of rode to water depth plus height of bow (*freeboard*).

More scope increases holding ability. While a ratio of 5:1 may be adequate for lunch in a sheltered spot with a good holding bottom, you'll want to increase it to 7:1 or more for strong wind and sea conditions.

Anchor and Rode Inspection
☐ Check anchor line for worn or frayed areas.
☐ Check chain for damaged links.
☐ Check shackles are in good condition and pins are securely fastened.
☐ Check condition of anchor.

Setting an Anchor

Lightweight-type anchor such as a Danforth holds well in sand, hard mud or soft clay bottoms, but are difficult to set in grass or rocky bottoms.

Bruce anchor holds well in most types of bottoms.

Plow-type anchor holds well in most types of bottoms.

Mushroom anchor is best for mud and silt bottoms. Unlike other anchors shown here, it depends primarily on its weight for holding.

❶ After checking area, approach anchoring spot slowly, heading into wind or current, whichever has a stronger effect on boat.

❷ Stop boat and lower anchor over bow — do not throw it. The end of rode should be attached to boat before releasing anchor.

❸ Let out anchor line as boat drifts downwind. If wind has too little effect, back boat very slowly while letting line run out freely. Avoid backing too fast, which could cause anchor to bounce along bottom.

❹ When a scope of 5:1 has been let out, wrap line around bow cleat and reverse slowly against it until it becomes taut. Once anchor is set, let out additional line as needed. To check whether anchor has set, hold a hand on the line while reversing to feel for any chatter or vibration from anchor dragging or bouncing along bottom.

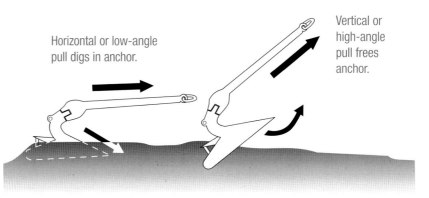

Horizontal or low-angle pull digs in anchor.

Vertical or high-angle pull frees anchor.

Most anchors dig into the bottom and hold best when pulled at a low angle to the bottom. A more vertical angle of pull can prevent the flukes from burying or even break the anchor free.

Retrieving an Anchor

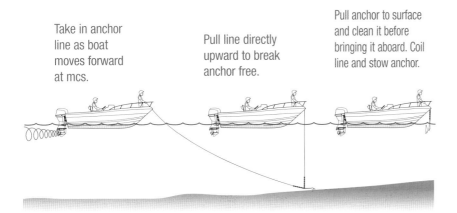

Take in anchor line as boat moves forward at mcs.

Pull line directly upward to break anchor free.

Pull anchor to surface and clean it before bringing it aboard. Coil line and stow anchor.

Tip...
A length of chain between the anchor and anchor line helps weigh down the line, which gives a lower angle of pull when setting an anchor.

Windlass. Larger boats usually use a windlass for raising the anchor, which can handle both line and chain. Although there are manual windlasses, most powerboats use electric versions operated by a button in the windlass or deck, or by a hand control. It's a good idea to run your engine while using an electric windlass to avoid running down the batteries. When lowering chain, use the brake to stop it, not your hand.

Keep clothing, hair and other body parts clear of the windlass. Never put a hand on the chain while the windlass power is on.

Hand Signals. The noise of engine, wind and waves makes it difficult to communicate by voice. Hand signals are a good alternative, but the driver and bow person should review them beforehand.

A windlass should be used to raise the anchor and its rode, not to break the anchor free.

Control button

Raise left arm with hand pointing to port (left) to indicate steer to port.

Raise right arm with hand pointing to starboard (right) to indicate steer to starboard.

Raise arm and motion forward to indicate go straight ahead.

Raise arm with closed fist to indicate stop.

Raise arm with palm facing aft to indicate reverse.

Leaving a Dock

Spring Line Departures. There may be times when strong wind, current or other boats tied to the dock make it impossible to use the back-away or straight ahead departure methods covered in Chapter 6. Knowing how to use a spring line will help in these situations. A spring line is a dockline that can work as a lever to turn a boat when you motor against it. The direction that a spring line runs from the boat defines whether it is an aft or forward spring line.

Springing Off with an Aft Spring Line. Spring lines that run aft from a boat are called *aft spring lines*.

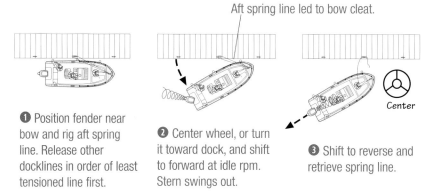

Aft spring line led to bow cleat.

❶ Position fender near bow and rig aft spring line. Release other docklines in order of least tensioned line first.

❷ Center wheel, or turn it toward dock, and shift to forward at idle rpm. Stern swings out.

Center

❸ Shift to reverse and retrieve spring line.

Doubling a Line

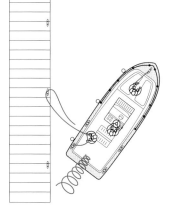

❶ Pass line around dock cleat and back to boat, making sure there are no knots in line that would snag on cleat.
❷ To release, let go of non-loop end, and as line slips past dock cleat quickly bring it in to avoid getting it caught in propeller.

Springing Off with a Forward Spring Line. Spring lines that run forward from a boat are called *forward spring lines*.

Forward spring line led to stern cleat.

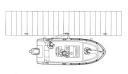

❶ Position fender near stern and rig forward spring line.

❷ Center wheel, or turn it toward dock, and shift to reverse at idle rpm. Bow swings out.

Center

❸ Shift to forward and retrieve spring line.

Doubling a Line. Doubling a dockline allows you to release a line from aboard the boat without any assistance from a person on the dock.

Returning to a Dock

Spring Line Docking. A spring line can be used to bring and hold a boat alongside a dock by leading the line to the middle of the boat's side. The large-angle approach described in Chapter 6 used this technique to overcome the boat being blown away from the dock.

Downwind Docking. With the wind (or current) from astern, any use of the engine for steering may cause a faster approach speed, which will require more distance and reverse power to stop the boat. Any increase in wind magnifies the problem. Once alongside the dock, the boat's windage can cause it to rapidly drift down the dock or spin the stern out unless an aft spring line running from the boat's mid-length is quickly looped over a dock cleat. If the line is led to the bow cleat, the stern could swing out.

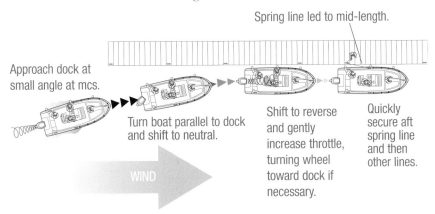

Spring line led to mid-length.

Approach dock at small angle at mcs.

Turn boat parallel to dock and shift to neutral.

Shift to reverse and gently increase throttle, turning wheel toward dock if necessary.

Quickly secure aft spring line and then other lines.

WIND

Close Quarters Docking. Before making this approach, stop and carefully check wind and current conditions. If you feel uncomfortable about the dock space, look for another location. Use the aft spring line to bring the boat alongside and to ensure the boat stops short of the boat in front. Pass the loop end of the spring line to a person on the dock, telling him which dock cleat to use, while you adjust the length of the line from the boat.

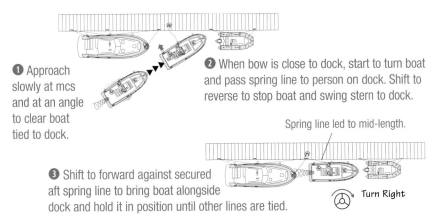

❶ Approach slowly at mcs and at an angle to clear boat tied to dock.

❷ When bow is close to dock, start to turn boat and pass spring line to person on dock. Shift to reverse to stop boat and swing stern to dock.

Spring line led to mid-length.

❸ Shift to forward against secured aft spring line to bring boat alongside dock and hold it in position until other lines are tied.

Turn Right

Docking with a Bow Thruster

❶ Approach dock at appropriate angle for wind/current conditions at mcs. Use bow thruster to adjust angle if necessary.
❷ Shift into neutral when about 1/2 to 1 boat length away from dock.
❸ When bow is close to dock, use bow thruster to turn boat parallel to dock, while shifting to reverse or forward gear to keep boat close to dock.

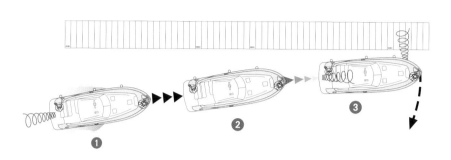

Returning to a Slip

Crosswind Approach

❶ Turn boat so it is parallel to and upwind of slip.
❷ Adjust speed with gearshift to maneuver boat into slip, using forward momentum and windage.
❸ Shift to reverse to stop boat. Secure docklines.

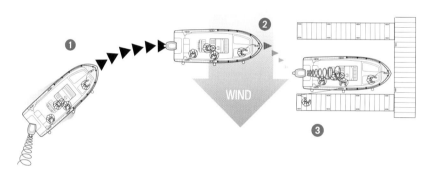

Backing into a Slip

❶ Make 90-degree turn just to windward of slip.
❷ Pass close to windward piling as you back into slip so a person can put loop end of bow line over piling (or pick up line attached to piling).
❸ Pass stern line to cleat on slip when stern gets close enough to slip.
❹ Once these two lines are attached, pull boat back with bow line to pass second bow line over (or pick up line from) other piling and then back in to rig the second stern line.

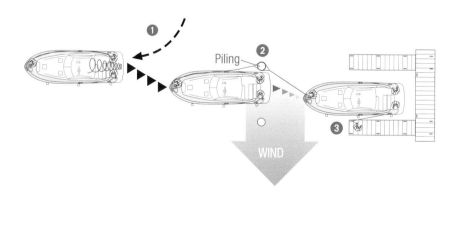

Mooring

Moorings typically have a large buoy that is attached to an anchor on the bottom with chain. They often have a floating line *(pennant)*, sometimes rigged with a pickup pole, which you can grab to bring the pennant aboard. If there is no pole or you cannot reach it, you will need a boat hook. Some moorings may not have a pennant and you'll need to tie a stout line to the chain or the ring on the bottom of the buoy, using two round turns to reduce chafe. Buoys may have a ring on top, but before tying onto it make sure a metal rod connects it to the bottom ring. A ring attached only to the buoy's surface could rip off.

Departure

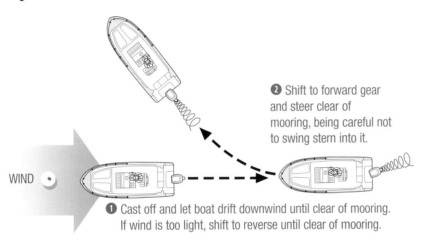

❷ Shift to forward gear and steer clear of mooring, being careful not to swing stern into it.

WIND

❶ Cast off and let boat drift downwind until clear of mooring. If wind is too light, shift to reverse until clear of mooring.

Picking Up a Mooring. The driver should approach the mooring with it on his side of the boat to keep it in sight throughout the approach. If the driver loses sight of the mooring, the bow person should use hand signals and a boat hook to direct the driver.

Coming Alongside an Anchored Boat

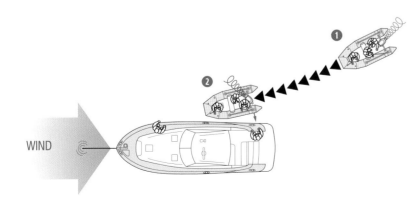

WIND

Picking Up a Mooring

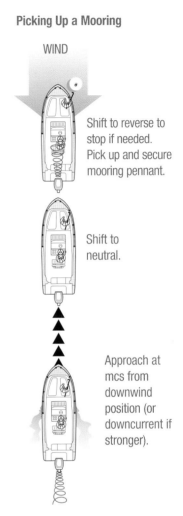

WIND

Shift to reverse to stop if needed. Pick up and secure mooring pennant.

Shift to neutral.

Approach at mcs from downwind position (or downcurrent if stronger).

❶ Determine swing behavior of anchored boat and approach at an appropriate angle at mcs. When boat is about half to one boat length away, make smooth turn to bring boat parallel to anchored boat and shift to neutral.

❷ Reverse to stop boat. If necessary, increase throttle to accelerate swing, especially if anchored boat starts to swing away. Shift to neutral and tie up.

Effect of Wind Shifts on Coming Alongside. Generally, anchored boats point into the wind unless the current is stronger. Before making your approach, determine the amount and quickness of the anchored boat's oscillations and adjust your approach angle accordingly.

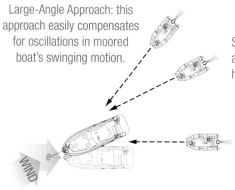

Large-Angle Approach: this approach easily compensates for oscillations in moored boat's swinging motion.

Small-Angle Approach: if boat swings any further, you will have to stop and hold position until it swings back.

Straight Approach: will have to stop and hold position until boat swings back.

WIND

Locks

Locks are a means of allowing a boat to pass around a dam or from one different water level to another. Many locks have an on-duty lockmaster who controls all movement through the locks, sometimes using horn or light signals and/or VHF radio.

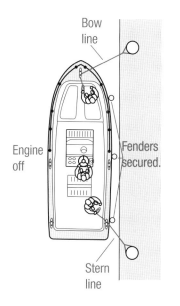

Bow line

Engine off

Fenders secured.

Stern line

Maintain tension on bow and stern lines as the water level in the lock changes.

Light Signals
Green = enter lock
Yellow (often flashing) = prepare to move into lock
Red = do not enter

Horn Signals
One long blast = enter lock
One short blast = leave lock

A boat entering a lock should have fenders in place and adequate lengths of line coiled and ready to use. Boats may "lock-through" alongside a lock wall or in the center of the chamber tied off on both sides. Once secured, the engine should be turned off. With large changes of water level, the water in the lock may become quite turbulent when the water rises in the lock. Never depend on holding onto or fending off the lock wall with hands or feet.

High-Speed Maneuvering

When running at high speed, a boat is less affected by wind. Other considerations become important, such as sea conditions, wake from other boats and semi-submerged objects in the water. Hard impact at high speed can cause loss of steering control, damage to powertrain or hull and possible injury to occupants. Any gear that is not carefully stowed or secured can take flight when maneuvering at high speeds, especially through waves. Constant alertness, a safe attitude and quick responses by the driver are at a premium. To be able to respond promptly, keep a hand on the throttle at all times.

During turning maneuvers, thrust from the propeller causes the boat to roll on its longitudinal axis. As the speed and tightness of a turn increases, the amount of roll increases. In a sharp turn with the boat rolled at a substantial angle, propellers on outboards and stern drives are closer to the water surface, which can result in air being drawn into its blades (sometimes referred to as *ventilation*). When this occurs, there will be a sudden increase in engine rpm and loss of propeller power. To avoid possible damage to the engine and drive system, the rate of turn and/or speed should be reduced immediately. If the drive unit is trimmed up too much, it can aggravate this problem.

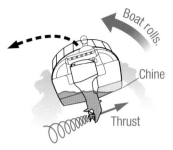

As a boat rolls in a tight turn, it also slides sideways. If the boat has a chine and hits a wave sideways at high speed, it could trip over its chine or throw someone overboard.

High-Speed Safety Tips
- *All occupants should be in seats and/or have a secure grip on boat.*
- *Attach lanyard to driver, if applicable.*
- *Keep one hand on the throttle and the other on the steering wheel.*
- *Maintain an alert lookout; don't get distracted.*
- *Use moderate and measured steering adjustments.*
- *Warn occupants of sudden changes in speed and direction.*
- *Avoid abrupt stops.*
- *If in doubt, slow down.*

Operating a Waterskiing Boat

In addition to the high-speed boathandling skills described above, safe waterskiing requires additional considerations and skills. States and local jurisdictions may have additional requirements and limitations.

Equipment Considerations:
- Appropriate USCG approved, high-impact PFD (inflatable type is not suitable) must be worn by a skier.
- Towline: typically 75 feet, but maximum length limitation may vary depending on use (check local/state regulations).

Turn Left

Turn Right

OK

Speed OK

Driving Tips:
- *Wait for a "start" signal from a skier before accelerating and steer straight.*
- *Use a lower speed for inexperienced skiers.*
- *Make wide turns.*
- *Return immediately once a skier has fallen or dropped off.*
- *Make your approach slowly when operating near a person in the water, being especially careful with a propeller-driven boat.*
- *Turn off the engine when dropping off or picking up a skier in the water.*
- *Allow a 200-foot wide corridor (or twice the length of the towline) for the skier to avoid accidents.*

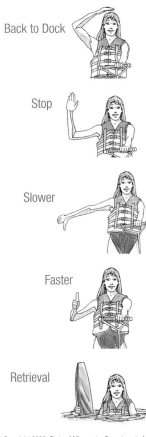

Back to Dock

Stop

Slower

Faster

Retrieval

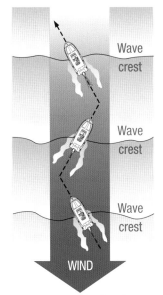

If your destination is directly upwind in heavy seas, you can "tack" (zig-zag) across waves for a smoother ride.

Safety Points:

- Have an observer in the boat to watch the skier and relay signals to the driver (many states require an observer even if a boat is equipped with a rear view mirror).
- Do not ski after sunset and before sunrise (Federal requirement).
- Use hand signals to communicate.

Heavy Weather Maneuvering

Smaller outboards are usually designed for use in relatively sheltered waters. If caught unexpectedly in bad weather or rough seas, position people and equipment as low and as close to the center of the boat as possible. Don't let water accumulate in the cockpit or bilge. A cockpit half full of water in severe sea conditions is a recipe for trouble.

Keep in mind that you want to work your boat through the waves while always maintaining control and minimizing stress on the boat. Avoid slamming into waves or falling off their backsides by making adjustments in direction and throttle to anticipate and react to changing wave conditions. Remember, one hand on the wheel and one hand on the throttle.

Running against Wind and Waves. As waves increase in size, it is usually better not to pound straight into them, but to cross them at an angle to produce an easier ride for the boat and its occupants. This angle will vary from 10 degrees to 45 degrees, depending on the size of the waves. Often waves seem to come in a recurring pattern with a couple of smaller ones followed by a larger one, then a couple of smaller ones followed by a larger one, etc. Sometimes, it is just a matter of slowing down a little to let the boat ride over the large wave. Other times, you may have to increase your angle to the large wave and slow down. Once it passes, you can go back to your previous direction and throttle setting.

Running with Wind and Waves. When strong winds and large waves are coming from behind, there is a risk of running down the front side of a wave and burying the bow in the backside of the next

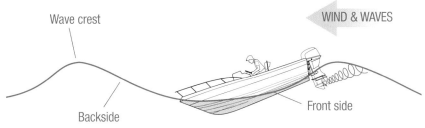

Wave crest

WIND & WAVES

Backside

Front side

Bow buries in backside of wave.

wave. If it appears that the bow will hit and possibly bury, immediately throttle back. If no action is taken, the boat could continue to submarine under the wave, swamping the boat. If the boat buries its bow at an angle, people could be thrown out or the boat could corkscrew and flip over. To avoid this situation, run at slower speed to match the speed of the waves, maintaining a position just behind the crest.

Safety Tip for Inlets...
Large waves are frequently encountered in inlets, especially with an outgoing (ebbing) current and wind blowing onshore. If the inlet is too rough, it's safer to remain offshore and wait for slack water or less wind.

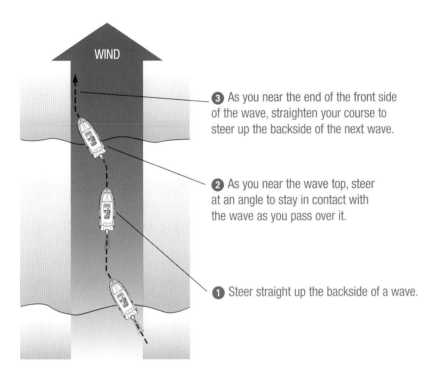

WIND

3 As you near the end of the front side of the wave, straighten your course to steer up the backside of the next wave.

2 As you near the wave top, steer at an angle to stay in contact with the wave as you pass over it.

1 Steer straight up the backside of a wave.

Another situation to avoid is jumping off wave tops at high speed and making a hard landing, which could injure people on board or cause damage to the boat. You should run at a slower speed to get a softer ride. In large waves, which are widely spaced apart and not breaking, you can work your way through them by angling over the wave top to avoid falling off them (above).

Running Sideways to Wind and Waves. Running sideways to wind and waves will give you a softer ride, but as waves get larger there is a risk of the boat rolling over or corkscrewing out of control.

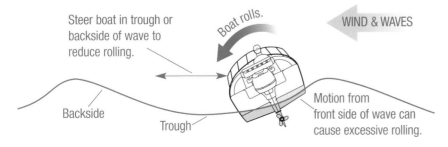

Steer boat in trough or backside of wave to reduce rolling.

Boat rolls.

WIND & WAVES

Backside

Trough

Motion from front side of wave can cause excessive rolling.

Twin-Screw Maneuvers

Propellers on twin-screw powerboats typically rotate in opposite directions to counteract each other's side force (prop walk). If both throttles are set at the same rpm, the prop walk effect is negated and the boat will go forward and backward in a straight line. If one throttle is advanced more than the other, the corresponding propeller will create more thrust and prop walk, causing the boat to turn.

Advancing Twin-Screw Throttles. When advancing both throttles on a boat with twin screws, don't push simultaneously on both; instead "walk" the throttles forward by rocking your hand from side to side and working the throttles against each other. If you push against both, the boat could suddenly lurch forward with a burst of acceleration.

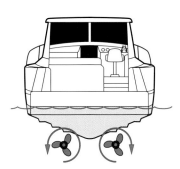

Typical rotation in forward gear

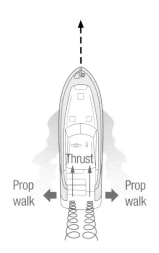

With throttles set at same rpm, the thrust and prop walk from each propeller is equal and opposite and the boat will run in a straight line.

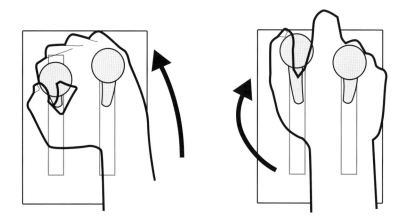

Turning Maneuvers. At slow speed, the gearshifts are the primary controls used to maneuver twin-screw powerboats with fixed propellers. In close quarters maneuvering, the rudders generally remained centered.

Controlling Your Turn. You can vary your turn by using different combinations of gearshift and throttle to change the direction and magnitude of the thrust and prop walk. If you turn the steering wheel in the same direction as the turn, you will tighten the turn. Experiment with these controls in different wind and current conditions in open water to learn how your boat responds. Your goal is to be able to control your boat with precision when maneuvering around docks and slips.

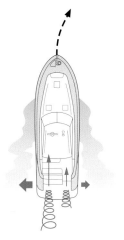

With one throttle set at higher rpm, that propeller produces more thrust and prop walk, causing the boat to turn.

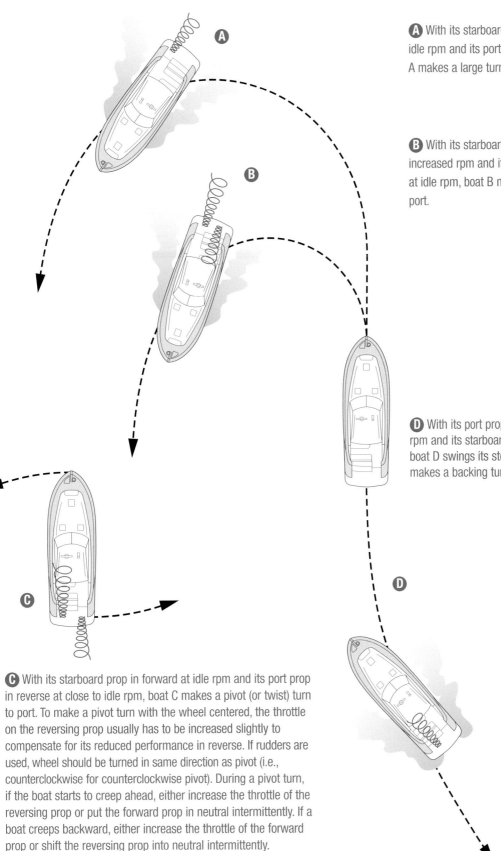

A With its starboard prop in forward at idle rpm and its port prop in neutral, boat A makes a large turn to port.

B With its starboard prop in forward at increased rpm and its port prop in reverse at idle rpm, boat B makes a tighter turn to port.

D With its port prop in reverse at idle rpm and its starboard propeller in neutral, boat D swings its stern to starboard and makes a backing turn.

C With its starboard prop in forward at idle rpm and its port prop in reverse at close to idle rpm, boat C makes a pivot (or twist) turn to port. To make a pivot turn with the wheel centered, the throttle on the reversing prop usually has to be increased slightly to compensate for its reduced performance in reverse. If rudders are used, wheel should be turned in same direction as pivot (i.e., counterclockwise for counterclockwise pivot). During a pivot turn, if the boat starts to creep ahead, either increase the throttle of the reversing prop or put the forward prop in neutral intermittently. If a boat creeps backward, either increase the throttle of the forward prop or shift the reversing prop into neutral intermittently.

Forward gearshift lever curves to port, bow turns to port.

Reverse gearshift lever curves to port, stern turns to port.

Many gearshift levers are curved inward at the top end. The bow will turn in the same direction as the top of the lever in forward gear, and the stern will turn in the same direction as the reverse lever.

Sideways Maneuvering. Many twin-screw boats with fixed propellers can be maneuvered sideways with varying degrees of effectiveness dependent on hull shape and configuration of propellers and rudders. The method described here may not work for all boats. Practice this maneuver to determine what works best for your boat.

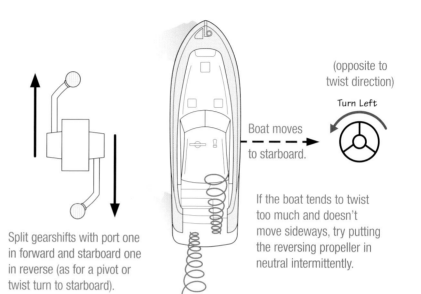

(opposite to twist direction)

Turn Left

Boat moves to starboard.

If the boat tends to twist too much and doesn't move sideways, try putting the reversing propeller in neutral intermittently.

Split gearshifts with port one in forward and starboard one in reverse (as for a pivot or twist turn to starboard).

Back-Away Departure. With twin screws this is simply done by reversing the propeller closest to the dock to swing the stern away from the dock and start backing away. Once the stern is clear, both propellers are reversed to back straight out. If conditions or other boats limit maneuvering space, then an aft spring line is coupled with a pivot turn to rotate the stern until the boat can be backed straight out.

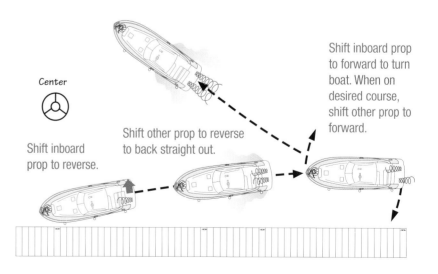

Center

Shift inboard prop to forward to turn boat. When on desired course, shift other prop to forward.

Shift other prop to reverse to back straight out.

Shift inboard prop to reverse.

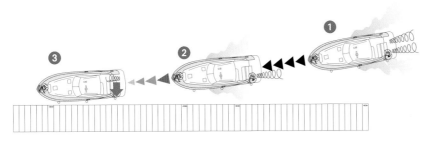

❶ Approach dock at mcs and at a small angle.
❷ Shift outboard prop to neutral to start a smooth turn to bring boat almost parallel and close to dock. Rudder may be used, but is optional. Shift inboard prop to neutral before end of turn.
❸ Shift outboard prop to reverse to swing stern and stop boat. Reverse other prop, if necessary.

Docking. A twin-screw powerboat can be easily docked on either side because prop walk is equally effective for both sides. With the standard propeller configuration (inboard rotation in reverse) prop walk from a reversing propeller will move the stern to the opposite side.

Backing into a Slip

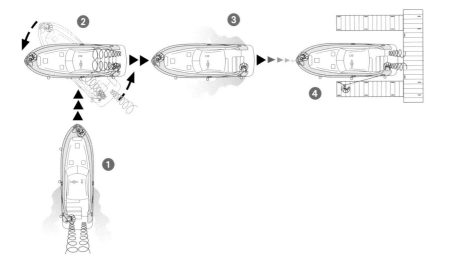

❶ Approach at mcs.
❷ Make a pivot turn to line up boat stern first to slip.
❸ Shift both props to reverse at idle rpm to back into slip. Control speed and direction by shifting props to neutral as needed.
❹ Stop boat by briefly shifting to forward.

REVIEW QUESTIONS

1. Your boat has a two-foot freeboard. You wish to anchor on a windy day in 18 feet of water. Your anchor rode (line plus chain) should be at least _____ feet long.
2. A spring line running from the bow cleat to a cleat on the dock near the stern of the boat is called a/an _____ spring line.
3. The technique that allows a boater to release and retrieve a dockline without assistance while aboard a boat is referred to as _____ a line.
4. A sudden increase in rpm and loss of propeller power when an outboard is in a tight turn can be caused by _____ (air being drawn into the propeller).
5. Large waves are frequently encountered in inlets, especially with a/an _____ (outgoing) current and onshore wind. If the inlet is too rough, it is safer to wait for _____ water or less wind.

Answers: 1) 140 2) aft 3) doubling 4) ventilation 5) ebbing; slack

8. Equipment & Requirements

NOTE: Personal watercraft (PWCs) are subject to the same laws and equipment requirements that govern powerboats of the same size. There are additional requirements for PWCs which vary with each state. They include: boating certificate for driver, age and horsepower limits; speed limits within certain distances from shorelines, objects and swimming areas; noise levels; towing a skier; and wake jumping. Contact your State Boating Law Administrator for more information.
ONLINE... Directory:
http://www.nasbla.org/blas.htm

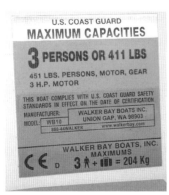

State registration numbers must be on both sides of the bow and lettering must be at least three inches high. The space between groupings of letters and numbers is equal to a letter width (except for "I" or "1").

KEY CONCEPTS

▶ Registration, documentation & numbering
▶ Hull identification
▶ Maximum capacities
▶ Safety equipment
▶ Federal regulations
▶ Pollution
▶ Accident reporting

Part of preparation is making sure you have equipment on board that works properly and conforms to federal and state requirements. Once you leave the dock, you'll be sharing the waters with other boaters and enjoying the natural environment. Safety and seamanship includes knowing and observing the regulations that help protect the waters and govern safe operation.

Registration, Documentation & Numbering

Registration & Documentation. A powerboat must either be registered in its state of principal use, or federally documented. The registration or documentation must be aboard the vessel at all times, and just as with an automobile registration, must be produced if requested by a law enforcement officer. If documented, the hailing port must be displayed on the stern and the documentation number must be permanently affixed to the inside of the hull. If registered, the state registration number must be displayed on each side of the bow of the boat in letters at least three inches high.

Hull Identification Number (HIN). Boats manufactured after November 1, 1972 are required to display a Hull Identification Number in two locations on the boat. Their primary number must be near the top on the starboard (right) side of the transom. In 1984 a second location of the HIN was required and it is located somewhere in the interior of the boat or beneath a fitting or hardware. Keep a record of this number to identify your boat in case it is stolen.

Maximum Capacities Label. All powerboats (except inflatables) smaller than 20 feet in length built after October 31, 1972 must have a legible U.S. Coast Guard capacities label permanently displayed and visible to the operator. For outboards the plate must display the maximum horsepower engine; the maximum weight capacity including passengers, engine and gear; and the maximum weight and number of passengers (passenger weight is controlling). Inboards require the same information except engine horsepower is not required. If the boat has no capacity plate, a rough guide is to multiply the length by the beam and divide by 15 to get a maximum number of people.

The Federal Boating Safety Act of 1971 and subsequent regulations specify the equipment a powerboat must carry based on a boat's length. The U.S. Coast Guard may impose a fine up to $1,000 for failure to comply with these requirements. It's smart to check your state's boating regulations in case they have additional requirements.

Personal Flotation Devices (PFDs)

At least one wearable Personal Flotation Device (Type I, II, III, or V) of appropriate size for each person on board is required. PFDs must be readily accessible, not buried under other gear or stowed in plastic bags in locked compartments. Any boat 16 feet long or larger must also carry at least one throwable type of PFD (Type IV) which should be readily available. PFDs must be U.S. Coast Guard approved, marked with a Type designation, and be in good condition. Regularly check all PFDs on board for loose stitching, rips, frayed straps or fabric and jammed zippers. Also ensure inflatable PFDs are maintained according to the manufacturer's instructions. Replace any that are no longer in good condition.

Offshore Life Jacket (Type I) is designed to turn an unconscious person from a face down position to a vertical or slightly backward position and maintain that position. The adult size provides a minimum of 22 pounds of flotation and the child size provides 11 pounds of buoyancy. The Type I PFD is suitable for all waters, but is the bulkiest and most uncomfortable to wear.

Near-Shore Life Vest (Type II) is designed to turn some unconscious people over, but the turning action is not as reliable or as pronounced as the Type I. Its adult size has a minimum of 15.5 pounds of flotation and it comes in four sizes based on the weight of the wearer. Type II is suitable for calm, inland waters and is relatively uncomfortable to wear.

Flotation Aid (Type III) is not designed to turn an unconscious person over and is used in a variety of sports such as sailing, skiing, hunting, kayaking, etc. It comes in a wide variety of sizes and colors and is the most popular and comfortable type of PFDs. Type III is good for a conscious person in calm, inland waters.

Throwable Devices (Type IV) are designed to throw to a person in the water to hold onto (not worn) until rescued. This Type includes boat cushions, life rings and horseshoe buoys.

U.S. Coast Guard approval notice (A) is sewn or stamped on the PFD and includes Type designation (B).

Type I PFD

Type II PFD

Type III PFD

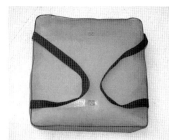

Type IV PFD (throwable)

Type V PFD (inflatable)

Type V "Float Coat"

Safety Tip...

If visual distress signals are not legally required for your area, it is good seamanship to carry them on board in case an emergency arises.

Special-Use Devices (Type V) are designed for specific activities and may be carried instead of another PFD subject to the conditions specified on the label. If the label says the PFD is "approved only when worn," it must be worn to meet the one PFD per person requirement. When inflatable Type Vs are inflated, their performance is equal to a Type I, II, or III as noted on the label (also check the label for USCG approval). Type V Hybrid PFDs have a small amount of inherent buoyancy in addition to the buoyancy created when their inflatable chamber is activated. The wide variety of Type Vs includes deck suits, "float coats," work vests and inflatable vests.

Inflatable vests are considered the most comfortable of all PFDs. Regularly check the CO_2 cartridge to make sure its seal hasn't been punctured. If it has, there will be no CO_2 to inflate the PFD. Always carry at least one backup cartridge. Once a year you should check your PFD for leaks by inflating it with the oral inflation tubes and leaving it overnight.

Signaling Equipment

Visual Distress Signals (VDS). All boats operating in U.S. coastal waters, the Great Lakes, territorial seas and those waters connected directly to them up to a point where they narrow to less than two miles are required to carry USCG approved visual distress signals. Powerboats less than 16 feet or boats participating in organized events are not required to carry day signals but must carry night signals when operating from sunset to sunrise.

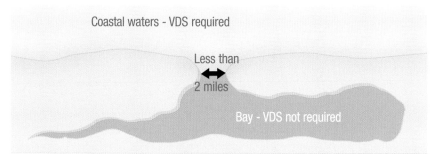

Coastal waters - VDS required

Less than
2 miles

Bay - VDS not required

There are a variety of visual distress signals available for day use, night use and for both. If pyrotechnic devices (flares, smoke signals, meteors) are selected, a minimum of three signals for day use and three signals for night use are required. All distress flares must not have exceeded their service life and must be kept in an accessible location. A watertight red or orange container labeled "Distress Signals" is recommended.

Day use only
- orange smoke signal
- continuous sounding of fog horn
- orange distress flag (black square & black circle on orange)
- slowly raising & lowering arms
- Intl. code flags "N" over "C"
- square flag above or below a ball

Night use only
- electric automatic SOS distress light (ordinary flashlight does not meet requirement)

Day/night use
- handheld red flare
- parachute red flare
- red-star meteor shells

All of these signals can only be used to indicate a vessel is in distress and requires assistance. If a vessel has a life-threatening emergency, it can use a "Mayday" call on a VHF radio as a distress signal. Chapter 9 describes how to make a Mayday call.

Signals to Attract Attention. Light and sound signals may be used to attract attention as long as they cannot be mistaken for distress signals, limited visibility signals or signals used when meeting another vessel (see Chapter 11 for information on these signals). A searchlight may also be aimed in the direction of danger.

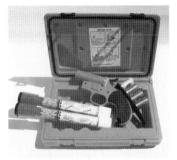

A watertight flare kit is recommended to meet visual distress signal requirements.

Sound Signaling Device. You are required to carry a sound signaling device that is capable of making an efficient sound signal. If your boat is 39.4 feet (12 meters) or larger, you must carry a bell as well as a whistle.

Navigation (Running) Lights

Any boat operating between sunset and sunrise, and during restricted visibility, must display lights. Lighting requirements vary considerably with the size and type of vessel (see Chapter 11 for more information).

Fire Extinguishers

Fire extinguishers are classified by the type of fire they are designed to extinguish and by their size. The letter indicates the type of fire: "A" for combustible solids like wood, paper, cloth, rubber and some plastics; "B" for flammable liquids such as gasoline, diesel, oil, grease and alcohol; and "C" for live electrical fires. Some extinguishers can be approved for several different types of fire and are labeled accordingly. The Roman numeral, which follows the letter, designates the size of the extinguisher: "I" being the smallest and "V" the largest. U.S. Coast Guard (USCG) approved fire extinguishers are required if any of the following conditions exist:
- inboard engine installed
- closed compartments or under-seat compartments where portable fuel tanks may be stored

Fire extinguishers should be readily accessible and mounted away from possible sources of fire.

Additional Equipment

In addition to the required equipment, most boats will need other items suitable to the intended use of the boat and available stowage space, such as:

- Anchor & rode
- Towline
- First Aid kit
- Heaving line
- Bailer/bilge pump
- Oars/paddles (for small powerboats)
- Tool kit
- Spare parts
- Boat hook
- Chart of area
- Boarding ladder
- Compass
- Flashlight
- VHF Radio and/ or Cellular Phone
- Spotlight
- Fenders
- Binoculars
- Docklines
- GPS

- double bottoms not sealed to the hull or not completely filled with flotation material
- closed living spaces
- closed stowage compartments in which combustible or flammable materials are stored
- permanently installed fuel tank(s), which could not be moved in the event of a fire or other emergency.

The minimum number of hand portable fire extinguishers (B1 or B2) required on a recreational boat is based on the overall length of the boat.

Length	No Fixed System	With Approved Fixed System*
Under 26'	one B-I	None
26 – 40'	two B-I or one B-II	one B-I
40 – 65'	three B-I or one B-II & one B-I	two B-I or one B-II

* An approved fixed system is an U.S. Coast Guard approved pre-engineered fire extinguishing system installed for the protection of the engine compartment.

Inspect fire extinguishers monthly to ensure: seals are intact, there is no physical damage, and that indicators are functional and reading in the desired range. Fire extinguishers should be placed where they are readily accessible and away from possible sources of fire.

Ventilation

All boats with gasoline engines are required to have a natural ventilation system for each compartment that contains an engine or fuel tank. A natural ventilation system consists of a supply duct for fresh air flow and an exhaust duct. A blower is required in the engine compartment for an inboard gasoline engine with a starter motor.

Air Circulation in Bilge and Engine Compartment

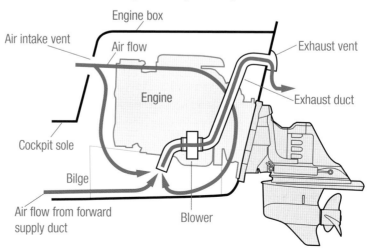

Backfire Flame Arrestors

All inboard gasoline engines must have a U.S. Coast Guard approved carburetor backfire flame arrestor on each carburetor to prevent the risk of fire if a backfire occurs. These flame arresters should be routinely cleaned.

Minimum Required Safety Equipment

A flame arrestor controls a backfire flame should it occur. Use only a flame arrestor suitable for marine use.

Equipment	Class A < 16 ft.	Class 1 16 to < 26 ft.	Class 2 26 to < 40 ft.	Class 3 40 to 65 ft.
Personal Flotation Devices (PFDs)	One type I, II, or III for each person on board or being towed on water skis, plus one Type IV for boats 16 feet and over.			
Whistle or a sounding device, such as a horn	Vessels less than 39.4 ft. (12 meters) must carry an efficient sound-producing device.		Vessels 39.4 ft. (12 meters) or longer must carry a whistle.	
Bell	Not required on Class A, Class 1 or Class 2 vessels.		Vessels 39.4 ft. (12 meters) or longer must carry a bell.	
Fire Extinguishers	One B-1 Type extinguisher. Not required on outboard boat less than 26', or boat is open construction and has no permanent fuel tanks.		Two B-1 fire extinguishers, or one B-II type fire extinguisher.	Three B-1 fire extinguishers, or one B-1 and one B-II fire extinguishers.
Visual Distress Signals (coastal waters only)	Required only when operating at night.	Signals for day and night use are required. Examples are: orange smoke signal (day) and S-O-S electric light (night); or three red flares (day/night).		

Water Pollution

The Refuse Act of 1899 prohibits throwing, discharging or depositing any refuse matter of any kind (trash, garbage, oil, etc.) into the waters of the United States.

Waste (Garbage) Management. Under the Provisions of MARPOL, the Act to prevent pollution from ships, a limitation is placed on the discharge of garbage from vessels. It is illegal to dump plastic anywhere in the ocean or navigable waters of the United States. It is illegal to discharge garbage in the navigable waters of the

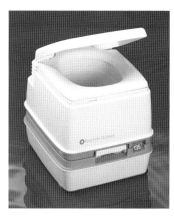

DISCHARGE OF OIL PROHIBITED
THE FEDERAL WATER POLLUTION CONTROL ACT PROHIBITS THE DISCHARGE OF OIL OR OILY WASTE INTO OR UPON THE NAVIGABLE WATERS OF THE UNITED STATES, OR THE WATERS OF THE CONTIGUOUS ZONE, OR WHICH MAY AFFECT NATURAL RESOURCES BELONGING TO, APPERTAINING TO, OR UNDER THE EXCLUSIVE MANAGEMENT AUTHORITY OF THE UNITED STATES, IF SUCH DISCHARGE CAUSES A FILM OR DISCOLORATION OF THE SURFACE OF THE WATER OR CAUSES A SLUDGE OR EMULSION BENEATH THE SURFACE OF THE WATER. VIOLATORS ARE SUBJECT TO SUBSTANTIAL CIVIL PENALTIES AND/OR CRIMINAL SANCTIONS INCLUDING FINES AND IMPRISONMENT.

"Discharge of Oil Prohibited
The Federal Water Pollution Control Act prohibits the discharge of oil or oily waste into or upon the navigable waters of the United States, or the waters of the contiguous zone, if such discharge causes a film or sheen upon, or discoloration of, the surface of the water, or causes a sludge or emulsion beneath the surface of the water. Violators are subject to a penalty of $5,000."

Portable toilets are often the choice for small powerboats. They can be easily carried on and off the boat.

United States including the Great Lakes. Boats of 26 feet or longer must display in a prominent place, a durable placard of at least 4 inches by 9 inches notifying passengers and crew of these restrictions.

Oil or Hazardous Material Pollution. The Federal Water Pollution Control Act of 1972 deals with pollution by oil, hazardous substances and sewage that may be harmful to the waters of the United States. The Coast Guard must assess a penalty of up to $5,000 against the vessel owner for every discharge, reported or not, of any quantity of oil that causes a sheen or discoloration on the surface of the water. In vessels of 26 feet and over, an Oil Discharge Prohibited placard of at least 5 inches by 8 inches must be placed in the machinery space.

If a vessel discharges oil or a hazardous substance in the water, the operator or owner must immediately notify the U.S. Coast Guard at a toll free number: 800-424-8802. A person who fails to notify the appropriate Federal agency of a discharge can be fined up to $10,000 or serve a year in jail, or both. The following information must be reported: location, source, substance, color, size, time observed.

Sewage Pollution. The Clean Water Act prohibits the discharge of untreated or inadequately treated sewage into the navigable waters of the United States, which includes coastal waters up to three miles offshore. The Act established "No-Discharge Zones" (NDZs) where the discharge of any treated and untreated sewage is prohibited. Freshwater lakes and reservoirs are NDZs. The EPA maintains a list of no-discharge zones, which is available online.
ONLINE... NDZs:
http://www.epa.gov/owow/oceans/regulatory/vessel_sewage/vsdnozone.html

Installed toilets (*heads*) on all vessels must be U.S. Coast Guard approved Type I, II, or III marine sanitation devices (MSDs), which are designed to treat, discharge or retain sewage. This requirement does not apply to portable toilets (heads). Type I MSDs are restricted to boats 65 feet long or less and treat the sewage to specified standards before being discharged overboard. Type II MSDs are required for vessels greater than 65 feet and have higher treatment standards for the discharged effluent than Type I units. Type III MSDs prevent the overboard discharge of treated or untreated sewage by pumping it into a holding tank. U.S. Coast Guard approved Type I and II MSDs are identified with certification labels. No label is required for holding tanks that hold sewage at ambient temperatures and pressures.

Pumpout stations are used to empty holding tanks and toilet dump stations are available for portable toilets. Information on the availability of these locations varies considerably from state to state. In some cases locations are posted on websites. Some nautical almanacs, such as Reed's, include pumpout station locations. You can also check with your local U.S. Coast Guard District or state boating office for the latest information on pumpout station locations and no-discharge zones.

A pumpout symbol identifies a pumpout station.

Negligent Operation

Negligent or grossly negligent operation of a vessel that endangers lives and/or property is prohibited by law. Grossly negligent operation is a criminal offense and an operator may be fined up to $5,000, imprisoned for one year, or both. The U.S. Coast Guard's Office of Boating Safety has issued the following examples that may constitute negligent or grossly negligent operation:
• Operating a boat in a swimming area
• Operating a boat while under the influence of alcohol or drugs
• Excessive speed in the vicinity of other boats or in dangerous waters
• Hazardous waterskiing practices
• Bow riding, and riding on the seatback, gunwale or transom.

Speed Regulations

Boats must be operated within posted speed limits at all times. When no limits are posted, a boat must be operated at a safe speed so it will not endanger others. This includes proceeding at a speed below wake-producing speeds (below 5 mph) when passing marinas, docks with boats tied alongside, restricted anchorages and swimming areas. You are responsible for any damage caused by your boat's wake. Navigation Rule 6 requires that at all times an operator must operate a boat at a safe speed in order to stop it within a distance appropriate to the conditions.

Termination of Use Act

This act gives the Coast Guard the authority to board a vessel at any time. If an unsafe condition is found, the boat operator must follow the directions of the Coast Guard Boarding Officer to take immediate steps necessary for the safety of those aboard. These steps may include direction to (a) correct the unsafe condition immediately; (b) proceed to a mooring, dock, or anchorage; or (c) suspend further use of the boat until the condition is corrected.

For the purpose of the Act, "unsafe condition" includes:
• insufficient number of Coast Guard approved PFDs
• improper navigation lights
• insufficient number of fire extinguishers
• overloading
• fuel leakage or fuel in bilges
• improper ventilation
• improper backfire flame control
• an obvious unsafe situation

Accidents

The highest incidents of boating fatalities occur in good weather, in the mid-to-late afternoon and predictably during peak boating periods such as summer weekends. While most non-fatal boating accidents result from collisions with other boats or objects, the predominance of fatalities occur because of capsizing and falling overboard. Over 95% of these fatalities were not wearing a PFD at the time of the accident.

A formal accident report must be submitted within 48 hours if a person dies or there are injuries requiring more than first aid. A formal report must be submitted within ten days for accidents involving more than $2,000.00 damage or the complete loss of a vessel. Accident report forms may be obtained at any office where boats are registered. The Coast Guard may impose a fine up to $1,000 for failure to report a boating accident. For more information on accident reporting, call the U.S. Coast Guard's Boating Safety Infoline at 800-368-5647.

Alcohol Abuse. Boating accident statistics continue to show a high correlation between boating accidents and alcohol use. Even in small amounts, ingestion of alcohol impairs vision, coordination, balance, awareness and judgment. It also has been shown that it hastens the body's heat loss thus shortening survival time in the water.

Because of alcohol-related boating accidents, most states have enacted "operating under the influence" laws. Generally a blood-alcohol content of 0.10% or more constitutes being legally intoxicated. Some states specify an even lower level. Most of these laws also allow an officer to make a determination of intoxication based on observation of an operator's behavior. Refusal to submit to toxicological testing is automatic presumption of intoxication. Importantly, the vessel must be underway before an operator can be considered to be violating the law.

Accident Reporting
Immediate notification is required if a person dies or disappears as a result of a recreational boating accident. The following notification should be provided to the nearest state boating authority.
• *Date, time and location of the accident*
• *Name of each person who died or disappeared*
• *Number and name of the vessel*
• *Name and address of the owner and the operator*

Rendering Assistance. A person in charge of a vessel is required by law to provide assistance to any individual in danger at sea if it can be done without seriously endangering the vessel or those on board. Failure to render assistance will result in a fine of up to $1,000 or imprisonment up to two years. A person rendering assistance in good faith to others who do not object is not liable for damages if he or she acts reasonably and prudently.

Diving Operations

Under Inland and International Navigation Rules, a vessel engaged in diving operations during the day may display a rigid replica of International Code Flag ALFA not less than 3.3 feet (1 meter) in height. This display is exhibited only by the vessel engaged in diving operations and signifies its inability to maneuver in accordance with the rules. It carries with it no special separation or maneuvering requirements for other boats other than to keep out of the way of the diving vessel.

International Code Flag ALFA (represents the letter, "A")

The Sport Divers flag has no official status in federal regulations. It is recognized by the Coast Guard as a flag indicating diving operations and, unlike the ALFA flag, it is used to mark the locations of divers in the water. Many states have enacted regulations requiring the display of the Sport Divers flag and specify standoff distances as well. A minimum of 100 feet is recommended but divers frequently stray considerable distances from their marker and separations of up to 300 feet are recommended in open waters. Like flag ALFA, the Sport Divers flag should be of rigid construction and conspicuously displayed. An operator of a vessel conducting diving operations should only display this flag to mark the site of diving operations. Having it painted on the topsides of a boat or flying the flag while proceeding out an inlet at 15 plus knots dilutes the meaning of the flag and has led to unintentional abuse by passing boaters.

Sport Divers Flag

Prevention of Boat and Equipment Theft

Theft of boats and equipment can be a concern. Some of this can be prevented by the following steps:

- Mark your Hull Identification Number (HIN) in a hidden location on your boat. On boats without HINs, it is often possible to "clear fiberglass" over a duplicate of the boat's registration number on the interior of the hull.
- Mark or engrave all valuable equipment with an identification number.

Prevention of Boat and Equipment Theft (con't)

- Keep valuables out of sight.
- Remove valuable equipment, including keys and certificate of number (registration) when you are away from your boat. Have a convenient boat "pack-up" kit that you take with you to your boat that contains all these items.
- Lock your boat and trailer to some immovable object such as a fence or a tree. For long-term storage consider removing trailer tires.
- Use a trailer hitch lock.
- Remove small outboard motors when not in use or lock them to the transom with a lock and chain.

REVIEW QUESTIONS

1. A wearable type of PFD that is not designed to turn an unconscious person over from a face down position to a vertical or slightly backward position is a _____.
   a. Type I
   b. Type III
   c. Type IV
2. All boats operating in U.S. coastal waters, the Great Lakes, territorial seas and those waters connected directly to them up to a point where they narrow to less than _____ are required to carry U.S. Coast Guard approved visual distress signals.
   a. 2 miles
   b. 5 miles
   c. 10 miles
3. The minimum number of hand portable fire extinguishers required on a recreational boat is based on the _____ of the boat.
4. A person in charge of a vessel is required by law to provide assistance to any individual in danger at sea if it can be done without seriously _____ the vessel or those on board.
5. A red flag with a diagonal white stripe is called the _____.

Answers: 1) b. Type III 2) a. 2 miles 3) overall length 4) endangering 5) Sport Divers flag

9. On-board Systems

KEY CONCEPTS

▶ Electrical systems

▶ Marine VHF radio

▶ Bilge systems

▶ Marine Sanitation Devices (MSDs)

▶ Fresh water systems

▶ Stoves

This chapter covers the basics of essential systems you will encounter on board most powerboats, but we suggest you also read and study manufacturers' manuals for more complete information on the specific systems used on your boat.

Electrical Systems

Most powerboats use a 12-volt DC electrical system. In smaller outboards, there is generally one 12-volt battery used for both starting and supporting other electrical systems, while larger boats may have a battery (or batteries) dedicated to starting the engine and another battery (or set of batteries) used to power lights, instruments, pumps and other equipment. On boats with multiple battery sources, a battery switch allows you to select the different battery systems. Whenever you start an engine or turn on lights or other equipment, you drain power from the batteries. The alternator on the engine charges the batteries when the engine is running, similar to the method used with a car. Larger powerboats may have a shore power outlet that enables you to plug into shore power to charge your batteries. If you have this type of outlet, your boat requires a battery charger to convert the AC (alternating current) shore power into DC (direct current) power.

Battery switch allows management of multiple batteries.

Most battery switches have four positions: #1 (battery one), #2 (battery two), ALL (turns on both battery systems), and OFF (shuts off all batteries). To start the engine, set the battery switch to the "start" position (either 1 or 2). If the starting battery's charge is too low to turn over the engine, set the switch to ALL (both), which may give you enough power to start it.

Shore power outlets provide electricity for charging batteries, if the boat's electrical system has a battery charger.

Larger cruising powerboats may also have a 110-volt AC electrical system to operate AC lights and appliances such as hair dryers, coffee makers, blenders, TVs, heaters and electric tools. To use the AC fixtures and appliances, you will either need to be plugged into shore power or have a method of generating AC power on board. This can be done by an AC generator (genset) or by an inverter, which transforms DC battery power to AC.

Battery Inspection

- Batteries and their boxes are secured and should always have a cover to avoid shorting the terminals inadvertently.
- Batteries should not be located in a confined space where accumulated battery gases may be exposed to an electrical spark and cause an explosion.
- Make sure battery terminals have no corrosion and cables are securely attached.
- Check the fluid levels of the batteries, if possible.
- Insulation on electrical wires is in good condition with no cracks or worn spots.

Battery Tips

- *Keep your batteries charged.*
- *Turn off electrical fixtures and equipment when not in use.*
- *Leave battery switches in the OFF position when leaving your boat (your automatic bilge pump should be wired separately).*
- *Don't reposition the battery switch with the engine running without first checking the electrical system manual to see whether this can cause a problem.*

Marine VHF Radio

The marine VHF radiotelephone system is a line of sight, Very High Frequency system and provides local marine weather forecasts, communication with nearby boats and marinas and access to emergency assistance. The VHF radio is limited by horizon, typically 10 to 15 miles for ship-to-ship communication and 20 to 30 miles for ship to shore, depending on the height of the antennas. At the low-power setting, these ranges are reduced. Handheld VHF radios typically have ranges of only a few miles.

Channel Designations

Each channel is authorized for a specific purpose. Check your nautical almanac for a complete list of channel designations. The channels of greatest interest to the recreational boater are:

Channel	Purpose
1, 2, 3, 4 – Weather	Provide continuous local marine weather forecasts, including storm warnings and watches.
9 – Secondary Calling Station	Is a general purpose, alternative calling channel in many areas where Channel 16 is congested. Check your nautical almanac or the Coast Guard to determine whether 9 or 16 is the channel to use for making initial contact. It is NOT an emergency channel. This channel is also the primary channel used at many locks and bridges.

13 – Navigational	Used to communicate navigational information between vessels, such as meeting and passing situations. This is often the best channel to contact commercial vessels.
16 – Distress, Safety & Calling	Used for distress and safety calls or initiating calls to other vessels and land stations. Except in an emergency, upon receiving a response, advise the other boat to switch to a non-commercial channel. Routine radio checks are prohibited on this channel.
22A – U.S. Coast Guard Liaison and Maritime Safety Information broadcasts	Is the principal channel for communication with the Coast Guard, except for distress and safety calls on Channel 16. It is monitored constantly and is the source for marine information broadcasts. To use Channel 22A, set VHF radio to the U.S. setting.
68, 69, & 71 – Non-commercial	Used for "intership" (boat to boat) and "ship to shore" (boat to land stations, such as marinas) communication for recreational boaters. Switch to one of these channels after initiating on Channel 16 (or 9).
70 – Digital Selective Calling	Restricted only to this use, which requires specially configured equipment.
72 – Non-commercial	Restricted to only "intership" communication for recreational boaters.

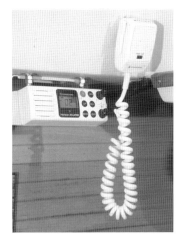

The console mounted VHF radio uses the boat's battery for power and has an installed antenna, which gives it greater range than the handheld model. Adjust the squelch control by turning it down just under the crackling sound.

Radio Communication Basics

• The high/low power switch on a VHF radio allows the user to select a power transmitter setting. Most communications should be attempted on the low power setting and only switched to high if needed.

• Use only those channels identified for recreational boating.

• Radio communication is public and shared. Speak clearly, be brief, and don't use profanity.

• Any vessel calling in an emergency always has priority over all other communications.

• When making an "intership" (boat to boat) call:

1. Initiate the call on Channel 16 (or 9, if it is the designated calling channel for your area).

2. Identify the boat you're calling, then identify your boat by saying "This is" followed by your boat's name. EXAMPLE: "Resolute, Resolute, Resolute. This is Sabino. Over." "Over" indicates this is the end of my transmission and a response is desired.

3. Once contact is made, you must switch to a non-commercial channel, if both of you are recreational boaters.

The procedures for calling a shore station are the same, except if the shore station has an assigned operating channel, call them on that frequency instead of Channel 16 (or 9).

• When ending a call:

1. Each boat must give its name followed by the word "Out." "Out" indicates this is the end of my transmission and no response is desired or required. Do not use "over" or "over and out." EXAMPLE: "This is Resolute. Out." and "Sabino. Out."

For best results with the handheld VHF radio have a fully charged battery pack. Remember to turn off the power when not in use.

This lever-type drain plug can be easily removed to drain the bilge and secured in place to prevent loosening from vibration.

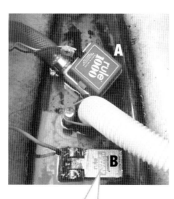

Electric bilge pumps (A) are automatically activated by a float switch (B).

Smaller powerboats often have manual bilge pumps.

2. Both boats switch back to Channel 16 (or 9).

- "MAYDAY" distress calls are made when a vessel or person is threatened by grave and imminent danger requiring immediate assistance. To send a distress call, repeat "MAYDAY" three times followed by "This is" and repeat your boat's name three times. EXAMPLE: "MAYDAY, MAYDAY, MAYDAY. This is Lead Balloon, Lead Balloon, Lead Balloon." This is followed by your distress message — remember the three Ws: WHO you are, WHERE you are, and WHAT is your type of distress, assistance desired, and any other information to help with the rescue. EXAMPLE: "MAYDAY. This is Lead Balloon. We are one nautical mile east of Cape May. We are on fire and sinking. Two people are severely injured. Request immediate assistance. There are a total of five people on board. Boat is a 40-foot powerboat with white deck and topsides. Sending up red parachute flares and activating EPIRB. Over."

- "PAN-PAN" (pahn-pahn) urgency calls are made when there is a very urgent message concerning the safety (but is not life-threatening) of a vessel or some person on board or within sight. Use "PAN-PAN, PAN-PAN, PAN-PAN" instead of "MAYDAY, MAYDAY, MAYDAY."

- "SECURITE" (see-cur-ee-tay) calls are used to send a message concerning the safety of navigation or giving important meteorological warnings. SECURITE is spoken three times.

Bilge Systems

The bilge is located along the inside bottom of a boat where water from leaks, rain, waves or washdowns may collect. Many powerboats have a drainage system that allows you to drain either the entire bilge or various compartments in the bilge through drain holes in the transom when the boat is hauled out of the water. These are closed with drain plugs, which are either screwed in or locked in place by expanding the plug using a lever. Make sure these plugs are secured before launching your boat.

Boats that have a battery system for lights and electrical equipment usually have an electric bilge pump. Most of these pumps have a float switch that automatically activates the pump once water in the bilge reaches a certain level.

Small boats typically use manual bilge pumps or bailing scoops, but larger boats with electric pumps also carry manual pumps in case the batteries run down or for emergencies.

There are drainage systems on some small boats that allow bilge water to exit the stern when the boat is running at a speed. Boats with this system will have drain plugs accessible from inside the boat that seal the drains when the boat is below self-bailing speed.

Bilge System Inspection
- Check the bilge regularly for any unusual amount of water.
- Carry extra drain plugs.
- Stow manual bilge pumps or pump handles in a readily accessible location.
- Keep intake screens on bilge pumps free of debris.
- Make sure float switch on electric pump operates freely and is not clogged with debris.

Marine Sanitation Devices (MSDs)

Marine toilets (heads) generally do not have the capacity of toilets in the home. They tolerate less toilet paper and NO foreign objects. Typically, a manual pump is used to pump raw-water (seawater) into the head and pump the discharge into a holding tank or treatment device. On larger boats, an electric pump may replace the manual one. No matter what type of system is used, always explain its operation to everyone on board.

Electrically operated heads use a push-button to flush.

Head Operation
❶ Open raw-water (seawater) seacock.
❷ For manually operated heads, depress hand or foot lever and pump a small amount of water into bowl before using.

Manual heads may have a foot lever instead of a hand lever or twist knob. Depress the pedal to let water in and release it to stop.

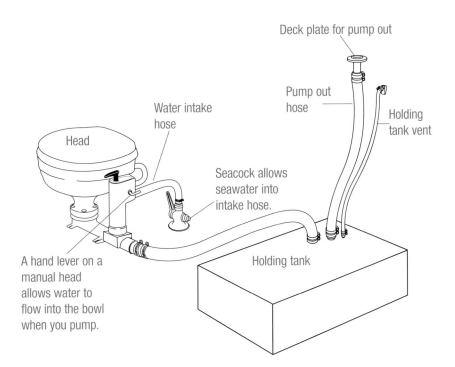

Deck plate for pump out

Pump out hose

Water intake hose

Holding tank vent

Head

Seacock allows seawater into intake hose.

A hand lever on a manual head allows water to flow into the bowl when you pump.

Holding tank

Larger boats often have a pressurized water system with "on/off" faucets (above) and may also have a manual pump water system (operated by black handle shown) to conserve water. Some manual pumps are operated by pumping a foot lever (below). A foot pump lets you use both hands while pumping.

❸ For manually operated head, depress hand or foot lever to flush and pump until bowl is clear. Pump additional strokes to make sure the discharge line is clear.

❹ Release hand or foot lever and pump bowl dry.

❺ Close valves, seacock(s) and toilet lid after use.

MSD Tips
• *Make sure all valves and seacock(s) are open before using.*
• *Stop pumping if you encounter resistance.*
• *Don't put anything in the head except a small amount of toilet paper or something that has been swallowed first.*
• *Close valves and seacock(s) after using.*
• *Leave area clean for the next person.*

Fresh Water System

Boats carry a limited amount of fresh water in one or several water tanks, depending on the size of the boat. As a result, water conservation is always a consideration, especially if you cannot conveniently refill tanks. To help conserve water, a manual water pressure system is typically used which you pump with your hand or foot to get water from a faucet. Larger powerboats with several tanks and a sufficient battery system usually have a pressurized system powered by an electric pump so that water comes out of a faucet whenever you turn it on.

Filling Fresh Water Tanks
❶ Close sink faucets so water doesn't run out when filling.
❷ Run the water hose for 30 seconds to clear debris before filling tanks.
❸ Check the deck fill plate to see it's labeled "water" before filling.
❹ After filling, tighten deck fill cap securely so water tank does not get contaminated.

Fresh Water Tips
• Turn off pressure water switch when everyone is on deck or retired for the night, and when leaving the boat unattended.
• Close valves and faucets when not in use.
• If the pressure water pump is running constantly, check the faucets, system and tanks for leaks. If the pump runs continuously, it will burn out once the water tank is empty.
• Conserve water.

Sumps

Drains from showers and iceboxes are usually below the surface of the outside seawater. They need to drain into a sump tank in the bilge

There is usually a deck fill cap for each water tank. Be sure you fill the one marked "water," not "waste" or "fuel."

that is emptied by a sump pump. If the tank is not pumped out and it fills up, water will not drain from the shower or icebox. The intake on the sump pump should be inspected and cleaned regularly to prevent it getting clogged by debris and hair. To avoid reverse flow in the discharge line due to siphoning, the line will frequently be looped above the seawater surface with an air breaker valve at the top of the loop or exit through the hull above the seawater. Keep the air breaker valve clean. If it gets clogged up, the discharge line may siphon seawater into the sump and flood the shower. Sinks are normally positioned higher than the seawater level and will usually drain directly overboard.

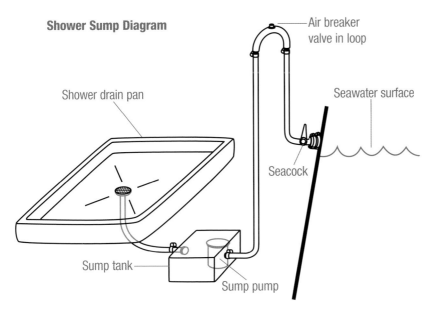

Shower Sump Diagram

Air breaker valve in loop

Shower drain pan

Seawater surface

Seacock

Sump tank

Sump pump

Stoves

Stoves on cruising powerboats come in several sizes and types. They can range from portable single-burner butane stoves and two-burner alcohol stoves (on smaller boats) to propane gas or electric stoves (on larger boats).

Alcohol Stoves. Alcohol stoves require preheating (priming) of the burner to make the pressurized fuel vaporize on contact and burn. When the burner is hot, the fuel can be turned on and ignited for cooking. Alcohol is a cool flame, it cooks slowly. Water will put out an alcohol fire.

Alcohol stoves are popular for smaller boats.

❶ Pump the tank and then open the valve to allow alcohol to run into burner cup.
❷ To prime the stove, close valve and ignite alcohol in burner cup.
❸ When the alcohol in the cup has burned out, open valve to the burner to access fuel. Ignite the vaporizing alcohol at the burner.
❹ When finished cooking, shut off valve and release pressure.

Propane stoves are efficient and convenient, but need to be used carefully. A solenoid switch (above) allows quick shutoff of propane tank.

Portable gas or charcoal grills are often used, but be considerate of others by not letting smoke or sparks from your barbecue drift downwind onto their boats.

Stove Safety Tips...
- *Locate fire extinguishers.*
- *Don't overfill the preheat rim of an alcohol stove.*
- *Shut off fuel when stove is not in use.*
- *Don't leave burner and oven controls on after you turn off the fuel supply.*
- *Don't forget to close the tank valves when leaving the boat.*

Propane Stoves. Propane gas heated stoves are easy to use, but because propane is heavier than air it must be used with care. Leaking gas can settle in the bilge and could be ignited by a spark.

❶ Turn on the tank valve and then the solenoid switch.
❷ Strike the match or starter before turning on the burner control.
❸ When finished cooking, turn off the solenoid and then the burners. Check that all controls, including the oven, are off.

Propane Safety System

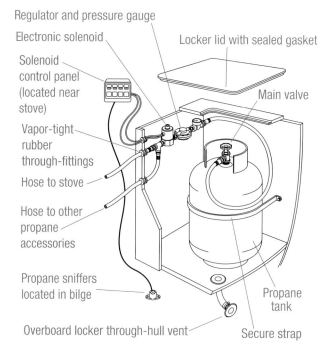

Regulator and pressure gauge
Electronic solenoid
Solenoid control panel (located near stove)
Vapor-tight rubber through-fittings
Hose to stove
Hose to other propane accessories
Propane sniffers located in bilge
Overboard locker through-hull vent
Locker lid with sealed gasket
Main valve
Propane tank
Secure strap

REVIEW QUESTIONS

1. *The type of electrical system most powerboats use for starting, instruments, pumps and lights is a _____.*
   a. 6-volt b. 9-volt c. 12-volt
2. *Except for distress and safety calls, when contacting the U.S. Coast Guard on a marine VHF radio, the preferred channel to use is _____.*
   a. 16 b. 22A c. 71
3. *When a person or vessel is in grave and imminent danger, the VHF distress call is preceded by the word _____ spoken three times.*
4. *Before using a manual or electrical pump on a marine toilet, make sure the raw-water _____ is open.*
5. *Propane gas must be handled with care because it is _____ than air and can settle in the bilge.*

Answers: 1) c. 12-volt 2) b. 22A 3) Mayday 4) seacock 5) heavier

10. The Environment

KEY CONCEPTS
▶ Weather   ▶ Winds
▶ Thunderstorms   ▶ Tides & currents

Weather, tides and currents play an important role in the success and enjoyment of a trip or a day's outing. Current weather conditions and forecasts can be heard on the radio and television or found on the Internet. You should also maintain a constant awareness of what is happening in the sky and on the water.

Weather

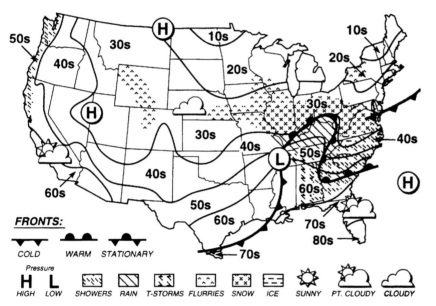

This newspaper weather map shows high and low pressure systems, fronts, types of precipitation, sky conditions, and temperatures. For more information on how to read weather maps (charts), see the weather chapters in the book *Passage Making**.

*order online at
www.uspowerboating.com

North American weather systems generally move from west to east. The speed at which these systems move depends on many factors. These include their strength, the location of the jet stream and the time of year. Typically, weather a couple of hundred miles to the west of you can be your weather for tomorrow. Current weather conditions and forecasts can be heard on the radio or television or found on the Internet. You should also get into the habit of using newspaper weather maps to help you get a picture of upcoming weather patterns.

High pressure system (H) usually indicates dry, sunny weather with cooler air and lighter winds than low pressure systems.

Low pressure system (L) is usually accompanied by a warm or cold front and inclement weather with stronger winds, rain and sometimes storms.

Barometers help predict the weather by measuring changes in atmospheric pressure.

Wispy, thin cirrus clouds often mean good weather for the day, but also predict an approaching change in the weather.

White, puffy cumulus clouds are often an indicator of good weather, and are typically seen after a cold front has passed through.

Towering cumulonimbus clouds, or thunderheads, are usually accompanied by heavy rain, strong winds and lightning.

Bays and harbors can be shrouded in fog when warm, moist air from the land meets cold water and cools below its dew point.

A front develops when colder, dry air meets warmer, moist air.

Warm fronts occur when lighter, warmer air rides up over heavier, cooler air. This front usually moves more slowly (about half the speed) than a cold front and brings overcast skies, rain and bad weather with the possibility of thunderstorms and strong winds. High cirrus clouds are first seen as the front approaches. After a warm front has passed, the air will be warmer.

Cold fronts occur when heavier, cooler air pushes under lighter, warmer air. It moves rapidly and is often accompanied by towering cumulus or cumulonimbus clouds, rain, strong winds and possible thunderstorms. After a cold front has passed, the air will be cooler. Tip: the symbol for a cold front can be remembered as icicles on a wire.

Personal Observation. Recognizing the patterns of weather systems and local conditions is an important part of your preparation and awareness on land and on the water. Be observant and learn to

Observation	Prediction
Sun and clear sky in the morning	Onshore winds during the day, and offshore winds (land breezes) during the night usually dying in the morning.
Thermal sea breeze	Increasing strength during the day as the land heats up and decreasing or dying at night as the land cools. Expect the wind to veer clockwise as velocity increases. In some parts of the country, increasing sea breezes will be accompanied by growing cumulus clouds.
Calm, overcast days	Continued calm and overcast, unless the sun comes out.
Cold and warm fronts	Showers or rain, changing air temperature, winds shifting in a clockwise direction. Cold fronts usually move faster than warm fronts.
High cirrus clouds	A warm front with rain and changing winds should appear in a couple of days. Clouds will get lower and more dense as the front gets closer.
Cumulus clouds growing taller (cumulonimbus)	Thunderstorms and strong winds.
Dark clouds approaching	A squall or storm

recognize the signals of impending weather from changes in wind direction, cloud patterns, air temperature and air pressure. The barometer measures air pressure and helps predict weather. A rising barometer usually means good weather approaching, a falling one warns of poor weather and a steady one indicates steady conditions. Rapid or large movements indicate major changes in the weather.

Thunderstorms. The familiar afternoon forecast of a 20% chance of thunderstorms can sound routine, but few weather phenomena can threaten boaters as quickly and as dramatically as a thunderstorm. They often advance on the heels of a sea breeze and if not detected early, can overtake you before you can reach safe haven. The first clue of their approach might be a distant, high altitude arc of cirrus clouds that often forms above cumulonimbus clouds. Any change in the color, shape or size of clouds means some change in weather is coming. The more pronounced the change, the more significant the weather. As a thunderstorm develops, the top part of the thunder-cloud becomes anvil-shaped and streams in the direction that the storm is moving. The wind ahead of a thunderstorm can be variable or steady, and may weaken and die as the storm approaches. When the roll cloud passes overhead, the wind will shift and blow violently with gusts that can exceed 50 knots. Heavy rain begins just behind the roll cloud.

A distant cumulonimbus cloud with a clearly visible anvil is probably going to pass to the side of you, but a rapidly growing cumulonimbus cloud with no visible anvil may be headed in your direction. Many storms develop erratic paths so their direction could suddenly change.

Squalls often accompany cold fronts and bring strong winds. If you see a squall line developing, it's time to seek shelter.

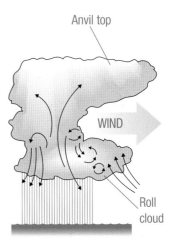

The anvil top of a thundercloud streams in the direction that the storm is moving.

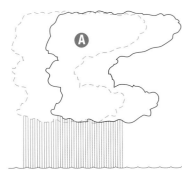

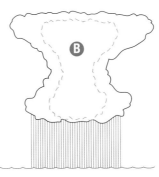

Both sides of cloud **A** are moving to the right of the boat, the storm should miss and pass to your right.

The left side of cloud **B** is moving to the left and the right side to the right, this indicates you are in its path.

The rough distance to a storm may be determined by timing the interval between a lightning flash and the associated thunderclap. Divide the time in seconds by five for the distance in statute miles.

Bad Weather Signals
- Increase in cloud cover and darkening skies
- Sudden decrease or increase in wind velocity
- Change in wind direction
- Lightning nearby or in the distance
- Thunder in the distance
- Gusty wind conditions

Winds

Winds are created from pressure differences in the atmosphere, blowing from higher toward lower pressure. Winds can be generated by major weather systems or local conditions.

Winds Around a High Pressure System. In a high pressure system, the pressure increases as you move toward its center, which will cause air to blow outward from the center. However, the turning of the earth causes this air to spiral out in a clockwise direction in the northern hemisphere.

Winds Around a Low Pressure System. In a low pressure system, the pressure decreases as you move toward its center, which will cause air to blow inward toward the center. The rotation of the earth will make this air spiral inward in a counterclockwise direction in the northern hemisphere.

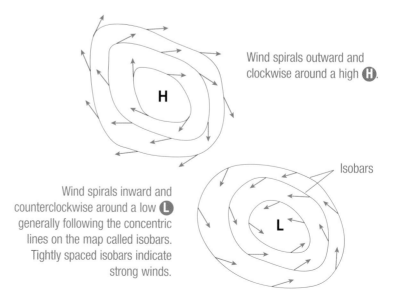

Wind spirals outward and clockwise around a high **H**.

Isobars

Wind spirals inward and counterclockwise around a low **L** generally following the concentric lines on the map called isobars. Tightly spaced isobars indicate strong winds.

Onshore and Offshore Winds. Local winds can be caused by the differences in air temperature over land and water. Sea breezes are formed as warm air rises above the land, drawing in cooler air from over the water. As the land heats up in the afternoon, the velocity of these winds will increase. Local offshore winds often occur at night or in the morning when the land has cooled and the warmer air over the water rises, drawing cooler air from over the land.

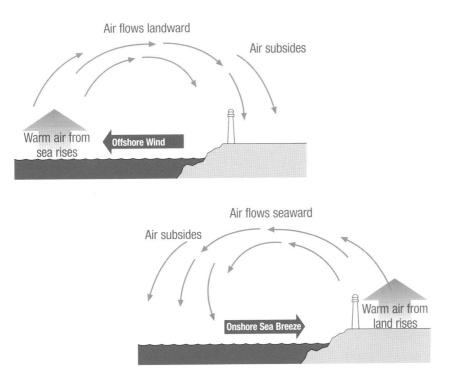

Topographic Effects on Winds. Wind direction and strength can be affected by local topography. For instance, on rivers surrounded by elevated land, the wind will tend to funnel down or up the river, following bends in the river.

Tides

Tides are the vertical movement of water and are caused primarily by the gravitational pull of the moon on the earth with the sun's pull a secondary factor. As the moon rotates around the earth, its gravitational force "pulls" the earth's water toward it. As the moon moves, so does the water level in most bodies of ocean water. Typically, there are two high and two low tides each day on the east and west coasts of the U.S. In the Gulf of Mexico, tides vary between two highs and two lows a day to one high and one low a day with very unequal tides in between. With a watch, a published tide table and a chart you can determine the depth of the water in which you are motoring or anchoring at any given time.

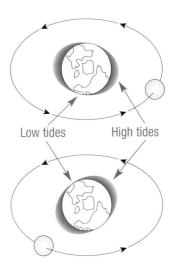

A tide table gives you daily information regarding the times of high and low tides and the heights of the tide at a number of locations. These are found in nautical almanacs such as Eldridge or Reed's. Some publications give a graphical representation of the rise and fall of the tide for each day.

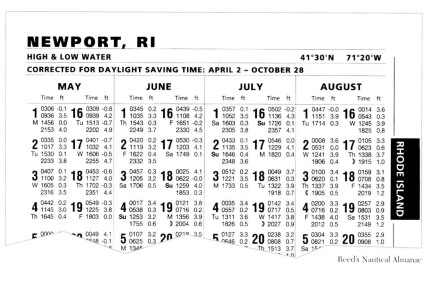

NEWPORT, RI

HIGH & LOW WATER   41°30'N   71°20'W

CORRECTED FOR DAYLIGHT SAVING TIME: APRIL 2 – OCTOBER 28

	MAY				JUNE				JULY				AUGUST		
	Time ft		Time ft		Time ft		Time ft		Time ft		Time ft		Time ft		Time ft
1 0306 -0.1 M 0936 3.5 1456 0.0 2153 4.0		**16** 0309 -0.8 Tu 0939 4.2 1513 -0.7 2202 4.9		**1** 0345 0.2 Th 1035 3.3 1543 0.3 2249 3.7		**16** 0439 -0.5 F 1108 4.2 1651 -0.2 2330 4.5		**1** 0357 0.1 Sa 1052 3.5 1603 0.2 2305 3.8		**16** 0502 -0.2 Su 1136 4.3 1726 0.1 2357 4.1		**1** 0447 -0.0 Tu 1151 3.9 1714 0.3		**16** 0014 3.6 0543 0.3 W 1245 3.9 1825 0.3
2 0335 0.0 Tu 1017 3.3 1530 0.1 2233 3.8		**17** 0401 -0.7 W 1032 4.1 1606 -0.5 2255 4.7		**2** 0420 0.2 F 1119 3.3 1622 0.4 2332 3.5		**17** 0530 -0.3 Sa 1203 4.1 1749 0.1		**2** 0433 0.1 Su 1135 3.5 1646 0.4 2348 3.6		**17** 0546 0.0 M 1229 4.1 1820 0.4		**2** 0008 3.6 0531 0.0 W 1241 3.9 1806 0.4		**17** 0105 3.3 0623 0.6 Th 1338 3.7 ☽ 1915 1.0
3 0407 0.1 W 1100 3.2 1605 0.3 2316 3.5		**18** 0453 -0.6 Th 1127 4.0 1702 -0.3 2351 4.4		**3** 0457 0.3 Sa 1205 3.2 1706 0.5		**18** 0025 4.1 Su 0622 -0.0 1259 4.0 1853 0.3		**3** 0512 0.2 M 1221 3.5 1733 0.5		**18** 0049 3.7 Tu 0631 0.3 1322 3.9 1918 0.7		**3** 0100 3.4 Th 0620 0.1 1337 3.9 ☾ 1905 0.5		**18** 0159 3.1 F 0708 0.8 1434 3.5 2019 1.2
4 0442 0.2 Th 1145 3.0 1645 0.4		**19** 0549 -0.3 F 1225 3.8 1803 0.0		**4** 0017 3.4 Su 0538 0.3 1253 3.2 1755 0.6		**19** 0121 3.8 M 0716 0.2 1356 3.9 ☽ 2004 0.6		**4** 0035 3.4 Tu 0557 0.2 1311 3.6 1826 0.5		**19** 0142 3.4 W 0717 0.5 1417 3.8 ☽ 2027 0.9		**4** 0200 3.3 F 0716 0.2 1438 4.0 2012 0.5		**19** 0257 2.9 Sa 0803 0.9 1531 3.5 2149 1.0
5 00~~~~ ~~~~ M 1345 ~~~~		**20** 0~~~~ -0.1 ~~~~		**5** 0107 4.1 M 0625 0.3 1345 ~~~~		**20** 0218 3.5 ~~~~		**5** 0127 3.3 0646 0.2 1~~~~ 1.0		**20** 0238 3.7 0808 0.7 Th 1513 3.7 ~~~~		**5** 0304 3.3 Sa 0821 0.0 ~~~~		**20** 0355 2.9 0908 1.0 ~~~~

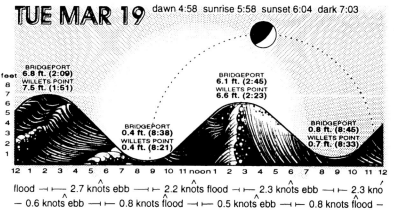

The heights from the tide table are added (unless they are shown as a negative figure) to the depth shown on the nautical chart to determine the actual water depth at a particular location at high or low tide. Be aware that weather conditions can alter these predictions

Currents

Current is the horizontal movement of water, and can be caused by a river's flow, tides, wind or ocean movements. The Gulf Stream off the U.S. East Coast is a well-known ocean current. In coastal areas, currents are caused by the tides falling and rising.

These photos, taken at the same location, show the difference between high and low tide.

Current affects all boats equally at any given instant. It can be compared to the situation where an adult and a small child are standing on a moving conveyor walkway, where both are moving at the same speed even though the adult is bigger and heavier. Traveling from one point to another, however, the effects of current on slow-moving boats is proportionately more than fast-moving boats because a slow-moving boat is exposed to the current for a greater length of time.

The "lean" and "wake" of this fixed buoy indicate a very strong current running from left to right (it leans the way the current is flowing). A small lean and no wake would indicate weak current.

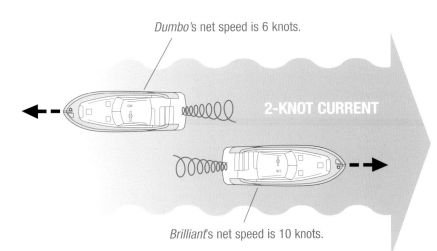

Dumbo's net speed is 6 knots.

2-KNOT CURRENT

Brilliant's net speed is 10 knots.

This illustration shows two powerboats motoring at 8 knots in a current of 2 knots. *Brilliant* has used the current to increase its speed over the bottom to 10 knots, while *Dumbo* has ignored it, making only 6 knots.

Tidal Current Table. Tidal currents are listed in current tables, including the times for maximum current and slack water (when tides change from ebb to flood or vice versa) as well as the general direction and strength in knots (1 knot = 1 nautical mile per hour). These tables are found in nautical almanacs, such as Eldridge or Reed's.

Tidal Currents Chart. For some areas, current information may also be presented graphically in tidal currents charts. These are published in sets of 12, relating to the hours before or after high water or slack water. The arrows indicate current direction and the numbers indicate current velocity in knots. *Flood* is incoming current and *ebb* is outgoing current.

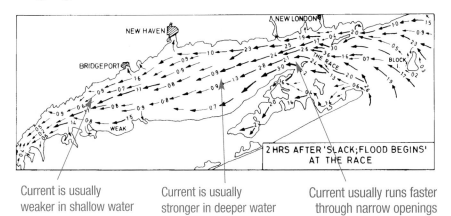

Current is usually weaker in shallow water

Current is usually stronger in deeper water

Current usually runs faster through narrow openings

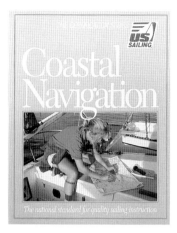

For more information on how to use tide and current tables, see the book *Coastal Navigation* *.

* order online at www.uspowerboating.com

REVIEW QUESTIONS

1. In North America, weather generally moves from _____ to _____.

2. As a thunderstorm develops, the top part of the thundercloud becomes _____ shape and _____ in the direction that the storm is moving.

3. Winds rotate in a _____ direction around a low pressure system.

4. Sea breezes or onshore winds generally occur at what time of the day?
   a. Morning
   b. Afternoon
   c. Night

5. Tides are the _____ movement of water and current is the _____ movement of water.

Answers: 1) west; east 2) anvil; streams 3) counterclockwise 4) b. Afternoon 5) vertical; horizontal

11. Navigation Rules

KEY CONCEPTS
▶ Inland Navigation Rules
▶ International Navigation Rules
▶ Maintaining a lookout
▶ Safe speed
▶ Navigation (running) lights
▶ Meeting situations

The fundamental purpose of the Navigation Rules is to help vessels avoid collisions. There are two sets of Rules. The *Inland Rules* apply to the navigable inland waters of the United States. These include the U.S. waters of the Great Lakes, harbors, rivers, bays and sounds on the shoreward side of the demarcation line, which defines the boundary between inland and international waters. The *International Rules* apply to the high seas and are known as the International Regulations for Preventing Collisions at Sea, 1972, abbreviated as 72 COLREGS. While the two sets of Rules are mostly similar, there are some notable differences in light and sound signals and situations in narrow channels. A complete set of the *Navigation Rules, International-Inland* is available at select marine supply stores or can be ordered from the U.S. Government Printing Office.
ONLINE... Online bookstore of U.S. Govt. Printing Office: http://bookstore.gpo.gov/
For *Navigation Rules, Intl.-Inland*: http://www.uscg.mil/vtm/navrules/navrules.pdf

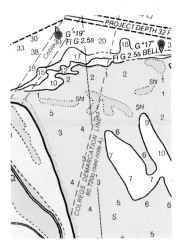

A magenta colored demarcation line depicts the boundary where Navigation Rules change from Inland Rules to International (72 COLREGS) Rules.

Maintaining a Proper Lookout. A vessel shall at all times maintain a proper lookout by sight and hearing and any other means available.

Safe Speed. A vessel shall at all times operate at a safe speed so that proper and effective action can be taken to avoid a collision or to stop within an appropriate distance. Safe speed is determined by visibility, traffic density, the boat's maneuverability, navigational hazards, water depth, wind, current and sea conditions.

Operating in Narrow Channels. A boat shall keep as near to the starboard (right) edge of a channel as possible. In shipping channels with adequate water depth outside the channel, a small powerboat should operate alongside the channel. A powerboat less than 66 feet long (20 meters) or a sailboat shall not impede passage of a vessel that can only operate in the channel. Do not anchor in a channel.

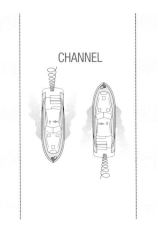

CHANNEL

The Inland Rules require that in narrow channels or fairways on the Great Lakes and Western Rivers, a vessel under power proceeding downbound with a following current shall have right-of-way over an upbound vessel heading against the current. The downbound vessel shall indicate manner and place of passing with appropriate sound signals.

Sound Signals

• A short blast is about one second's duration.

── A prolonged blast is from four to six seconds' duration.

For vessels in sight of each other:

● One short blast indicates *altering* course to starboard (International), or *intending* to alter course to starboard (Inland) when meeting or crossing.

● ● Two short blasts indicate *altering* course to port (International), or *intending* to alter course to port (Inland) when meeting or crossing.

● ● ● Three short blasts indicate engine is in reverse (although vessel may still be moving forward).

● ● ● ● ● Five short blasts = danger.

Other sound signals:

── One prolonged blast is sounded by a vessel nearing a blind bend of a channel or fairway, or when departing a berth.

For other sound signals consult the *Navigation Rules, International-Inland.*

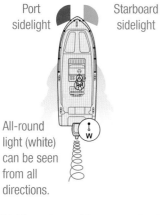

Port sidelight   Starboard sidelight

All-round light (white) can be seen from all directions.

Light requirement for a powerboat underway whose length is less than 39.4 feet (12 meters).

Sound Signals. Boats may provide information to other boats about their maneuvers through the use of sound signals. Nowadays, vessels may also use radio communication to make passing arrangements. This reduces the confusion generated by traditional sound signals in heavy traffic where it may be unclear who is being hailed. Monitoring radio communication is also an excellent way to gain awareness of vessel traffic. See Chapter 9 for information on channel designations of a marine VHF radio and their use.

Lights for Nighttime Operation. The Navigation Rules require "running" lights when operating from sunset to sunrise, during hours of restricted visibility or whenever it is deemed necessary. These lights can take many forms, such as sidelights, sternlights, masthead lights, all-round lights and towing lights. Their location and required visibility depend on the type and size of vessel. Some typical light arrangements are shown on pages 96-98. Refer to the Navigation Rules for additional light requirements for sailboats, Great Lakes vessels and vessels towing, pushing, fishing or restricted in their ability to maneuver.

Meeting Situations. A boat that is required to keep out of the way of another vessel is the give-way vessel. It shall alter its course in ample time and with an obvious change of course and/or speed to signal that the rule is understood and action is being taken. The other vessel is the stand-on vessel and should maintain consistent course and speed. However, it is every vessel's obligation to avoid a collision. If it becomes apparent that the give-way vessel is not maneuvering in time to avoid a collision, a stand-on vessel should then change course and speed.

TIP: To determine whether there is a risk of collision, you can take a bearing on the other boat. If the bearing remains unchanged, you are on a collision course unless one of the boats changes course or speed. You can take a bearing using a compass or lining up the other boat with an object on your boat.

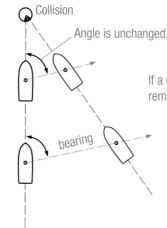

Collision

Angle is unchanged.

If a compass bearing to the other boat remains constant, you're on a collision course.

bearing

When boats are approaching each other, different Rules are used to avoid collisions, depending on whether they are meeting head-on, crossing or overtaking. These basic Rules are covered below.

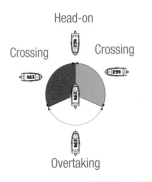

Crossing Situation Rule. When two powerboats are on an intersecting course, the boat on your starboard (right) side is the stand-on vessel, and the give-way vessel must alter course. Whenever possible, the give-way vessel should alter course to pass *astern* (behind) of the stand-on vessel.

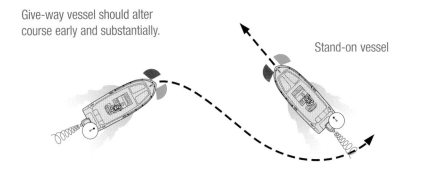

Give-way vessel should alter course early and substantially.

Stand-on vessel

Driver of give-way vessel sees these lights.

Driver of stand-on vessel sees these lights.

Tip: To quickly determine which boat must give way remember the colors of the port (red) and starboard (green) sidelights. If you see the red side of the other boat, think of it as a red traffic light signaling stop (or change course). If you see the green side, it's the same as a green light meaning go - maintain your speed and course.

The Inland Rules (Great Lakes and Western Rivers) require powered vessels that are crossing a river to keep out of the way of power vessels ascending or descending the river.

Head-on Situation Rule. When two powerboats approach each other, they should alter course to starboard (right) so that they pass port (left) side to port side and signal with one short blast. If you alter to port and pass starboard side to starboard side, the signal and response is two short blasts.

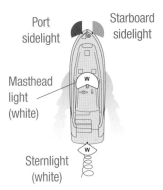

Light requirement for a powerboat (or sailboat using an engine) underway whose length is less than 164 feet (50 meters).

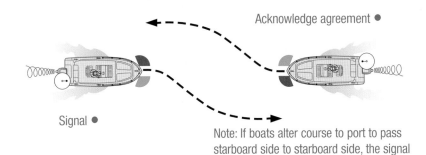

Acknowledge agreement ●

Signal ●

Note: If boats alter course to port to pass starboard side to starboard side, the signal and response is ● ●.

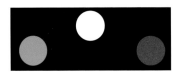

Drivers of both boats see these lights.

Driver of give-way vessel sees this light.

Driver of stand-on vessel sees these lights behind him.

Overtaking Situation Rule.   The passing (overtaking) boat is the give-way vessel and may pass to either side of the stand-on vessel.

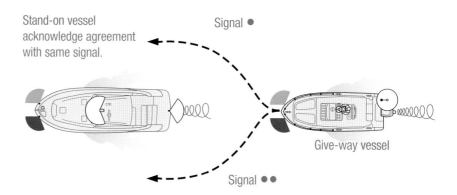

Meeting Situations When In Restricted Visibility. Restricted visibility can be caused by fog, mist, falling snow, heavy rainstorms, or sandstorms. In conditions where boats cannot see one another, a distinct set of Rules exist.

• Maintain a careful lookout.

• Operate at a safe speed for the condition and be ready to maneuver immediately. A rule of thumb is to travel at a speed at which your boat can be stopped within half the distance of the prevailing visibility.

• Listen for sound signals. If you hear a fog signal from another vessel forward of your boat's beam, you shall slow down to minimum control speed and be prepared to stop until danger of collision is over.

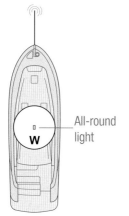

Light requirement for a boat being rowed: a flashlight is turned on in sufficient time to prevent a collision.

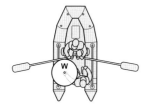

Light requirement for an anchored boat less than 164 feet (50 meters).

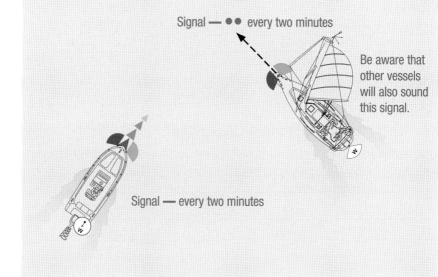

Responsibilities Between Vessels Rule. There are several types of vessels which a powerboat underway must avoid. These are:

❶ a vessel which is unable to maneuver as required by the Navigation Rules and is unable to keep out of the way of another vessel (this is called a vessel not under command). Examples: a vessel on fire or one whose engines won't operate.

❷ a vessel which by the nature of its work is restricted in its ability to maneuver as required by the Navigation Rules and is unable to keep out of the way of another vessel (vessel restricted in her ability to maneuver). Examples: a vessel dredging, or servicing a navigation mark or underwater cable.

❸ a vessel engaged in fishing with nets, lines or trawls that restrict its ability to maneuver. It does not include fishing with trolling lines.

❹ a boat using only a sail(s) for propulsion (engine is not being used) unless the sailboat is overtaking the powerboat.

Traffic Separation Schemes. Areas with a high volume of shipping will often have traffic separation schemes, or vessel traffic lanes, that are reserved for use by large vessels and those with restricted maneuverability. You should stay clear of these schemes.

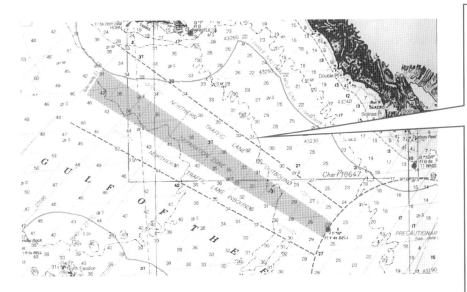

Homeland Security Regulations. All boat operators need to be aware of, observe, and operate their boats in accordance with Homeland Security measures, including Naval Vessel Protective Zones.

ONLINE... for Homeland Security regulations: http://www.dhs.gov/dhspublic/

Your duties in a Traffic Separation Scheme are as follows:

▶ You should keep well clear of Traffic Separation Schemes if convenient.

▶ If you need to join the traffic in a scheme, you should do so at the ends if this is reasonable.

▶ When crossing a scheme, you are obliged to cross at right angles to the traffic flow at your best speed.

▶ The separation zone must be crossed at right angles as well. Do not resume your course or run along inside it parallel to the traffic.

▶ You can go around the edge of a Traffic Separation Scheme without being subject to the above rules.

REVIEW QUESTIONS

1. The fundamental purpose of the Navigation Rules is to help vessels avoid _____.

2. The boundary between inland and international waters is marked by a _____ line which is shown on _____.

3. If you are in a crossing situation, the boat on your _____ side is the give-way vessel and must alter its course in ample _____ and with an obvious _____ of course and/or _____.

4. When the bearing of an approaching boat does not change you are on a _____ course.
   a. separation
   b. safe
   c. collision

5. In restricted visibility, a good rule of thumb is to proceed at a speed at which the boat can be stopped within _____ the distance of the prevailing visibility.
   a. quarter
   b. half
   c. twice

12. Basic Navigation & Piloting

KEY CONCEPTS
▶ Chart basics
▶ Position & distance
▶ Plotting a course & bearings
▶ Determining your position
▶ Using a range
▶ Navigation aids

The most important keys to successful navigation are visual. Boaters should be able to look at their surroundings and use what they see to help determine their position and a safe course onward. This chapter will cover a number of common visual elements, both natural and man-made, that can be used in conjunction with a nautical chart to help you navigate your local waters. We'll also include some of the fundamentals of plotting. Although electronic GPS navigation systems are widely used in boating, learning the old-fashioned fundamentals remains the basis of safe navigation.

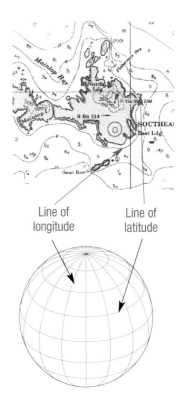

Line of longitude   Line of latitude

Lines of longitude appear parallel on the chart, but they converge toward the poles (see globe).

The Chart

Most nautical maps, called charts, use a Mercator projection to transfer the image of Earth's spherical surface onto a flat piece of paper. The primary advantage of a Mercator chart is that lines of latitude and longitude form an easy-to-use rectangular grid, which allows courses to be drawn as a straight line from one place to another.

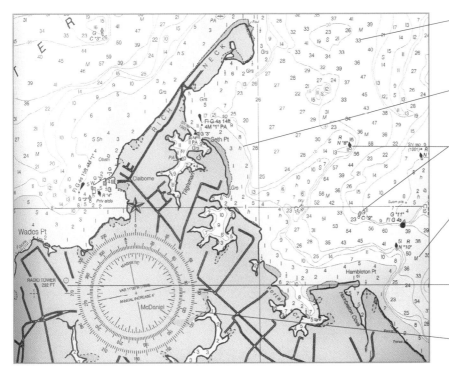

The small numbers scattered throughout the water are **soundings** or depths at low tide at those particular points.

A **contour line** follows a constant water depth. Areas of shallower waters are indicated in light blue.

Symbols are used to indicate **aids to navigation**. Red and green diamond shapes indicate buoys (see page 109).

Types of bottom are indicated, such as mud, sand, grass or rocky that you can expect when looking for a place to anchor.

Onshore landmarks, such as towers, can be used as navigation references.

A **compass rose** is printed on every nautical chart.

Soundings in feet

Heights in feet

Title block includes the measurement units used on the chart (fathoms, feet, meters, etc.), date when chart was updated and chart scale.

Nautical charts typically show areas of water and adjacent portions of coastline together with information useful for navigation, such as navigation aids (i.e., beacons and buoys), underwater features and landmarks on shore. Symbols and abbreviations are frequently used to convey this information and NOS (National Ocean Service) Chart No. 1 is a helpful reference for any notations that may not be familiar to you. The title block contains a great deal of important information, including units of *soundings* (water depths) and heights of land elevations. On this chart soundings are in feet. Other charts may have them in *fathoms* (1 fathom = 6 feet), fathoms and feet or meters. If fathoms are used, fathoms with a feet subscript may be used in shallower water. For example, a depth of 4 fathoms and 3 feet would be indicated as 4_3. If the soundings unit is in meters, the soundings will be indicated in meters and tenths of meters with the tenths shown as a subscript. Thus, 1.3 meters would be 1_3.

ONLINE... for Chart No. 1: http://chartmaker.ncd.noaa.gov/mcd/chartno1.htm

Position

Lines of *latitude* and *longitude* are used to define position on a chart. Both latitude and longitude are measured in degrees (°), minutes (') and seconds (") or decimals of degrees and minutes. On a chart, minutes and seconds have nothing to do with time, but are subdivisions of a degree. 60 minutes equals 1 degree and 60 seconds equals 1 minute. Make sure you know whether your chart is using decimals of minutes or seconds! Latitude is measured north or south from the Equator (0°) to the poles (90°) and longitude is measured east or west from Greenwich Observatory in England (0°) to the International Date Line in the Pacific Ocean (180°).

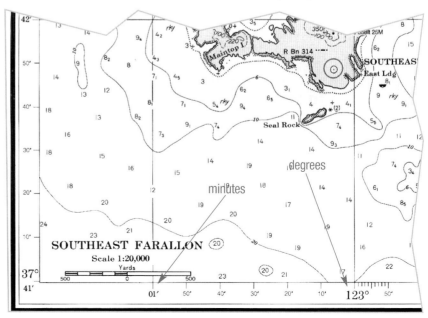

Plotting a Position

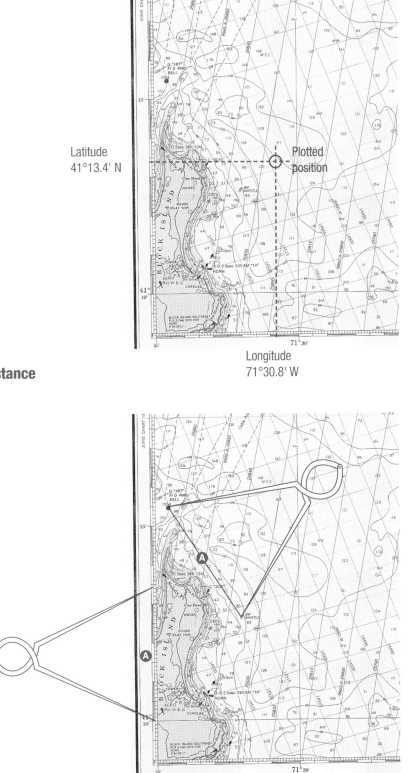

Latitude
41°13.4' N

Longitude
71°30.8' W

To plot a position of 41°13.4' North latitude and 71°30.8' West longitude, locate these positions on the latitude and longitude scales and transfer them to the position on the chart. This can be done by any of the following instruments: a drawing compass, dividers, parallel rulers or two drawing triangles.

Distance

If you wish to measure distance on a chart, you may use the distance scale located in various places on the chart or use the *latitude* — not longitude — scale. One minute of latitude equals one nautical mile.

To measure distance on a chart, open your dividers and use them to measure the span Ⓐ between two positions. Next transfer the span to the LATITUDE scale on the chart. Read the minutes of latitude and their decimal subdivisions (3.4' = three point four minutes). That is the distance in miles and tenths of a mile (3.4 nautical miles).

Compass Variation

Your compass points to magnetic north, but your charts are oriented to true north. The difference in degrees between your compass readings and true north is called *variation*. The amount and direction of variation will change depending on your location. The compass rose on your chart will indicate the amount and direction of the variation for your sailing area.

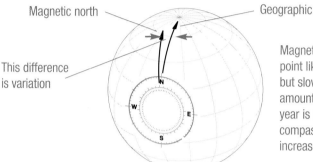

Magnetic north   Geographic or true north

This difference is variation

Magnetic north is not a fixed point like the true north pole, but slowly wanders. The amount that it changes each year is also indicated on the compass rose as an annual increase or decrease.

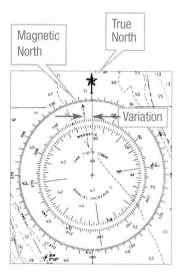

Magnetic North   True North

Variation

Compass Deviation

Your compass responds to iron or steel objects which have magnetic properties. The difference in compass readings created by their magnetic influence is called the *deviation*. For instance, a bag of tools accidently placed next to the compass can cause a deviation so that the compass reads 75 degrees when it should read 80 degrees.

Tips for Steering by a Compass. Steering by a compass takes a little practice. When you first try, the compass card never seems to want to stay still. When you try to catch up with it, it suddenly swings sharply in another direction. Here are some tips to help you master the art of steering by a compass:

- Know the position of the steering wheel for a straight course. Marking the wheel to indicate its centered position helps.
- Remember the boat turns around the compass. The compass card does not turn; it's always pointing in the same direction (toward the Magnetic North Pole).
- Don't chase the compass. A powerboat's motion can jostle a compass. Read the compass when the boat is stable, then correct your steering and check again.
- Don't stare at the compass. Look away frequently. Have a reference outside the boat (i.e., a landmark, buoy or distant cloud). Look at the compass and note the correction required, then turn the wheel as required. Look away periodically while the boat is correcting.
- Ignore body sensations: the fluid in your inner ear can cause erroneous sensations, especially in limited visibility.

The center post (lubber's line) on the forward side of your compass denotes the boat's bow and marks the direction (heading) toward which the boat is pointing.

Plotting a Course to Steer

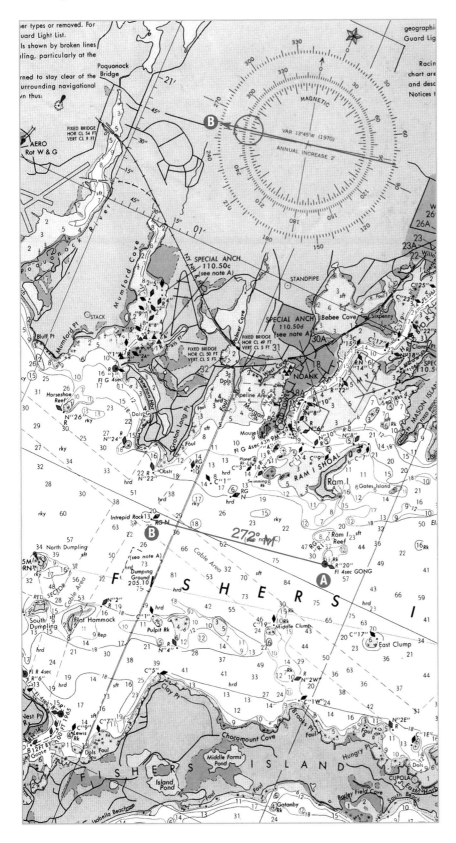

With a compass and chart you can determine your location as well as a course to steer. For instance, you are at point **A** on the chart and want to go to point **B**. Draw a line from **A** to **B**. Make sure there are no hazards such as rocks, reefs and shallow waters along the route. Now, transfer the line from **A** to **B** to the compass rose. The line has been drawn for you. Read the circled heading at the letter **B** on the inner magnetic circle of the compass rose. The heading is 272 degrees Magnetic (**M**), which is your compass course from **A** to **B**. To steer the course you have planned, just steer to the compass heading you have plotted.

Plotting a course with parallel rulers requires "walking" the rulers in parallel across the chart to transfer information to and from the compass rose.

The hand bearing compass (above) is more accurate for taking bearings because you can position the object just above the numbers on the compass.

Plotting a Bearing

An imaginary line joining a known point with the boat's position is called a *bearing*. In the illustration shown, bearing **A** has been taken of a chimney stack with a hand bearing compass. This compass reading is marked on the compass rose and transferred as a line running from the stack. Your position is somewhere on this line.

Determining Your Position

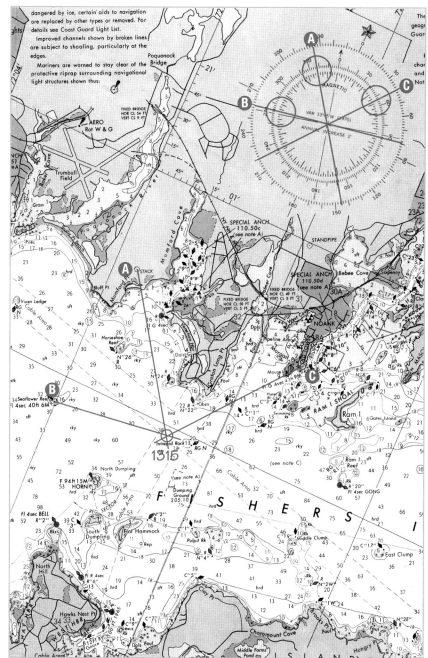

A bearing of **A** is taken with a compass.

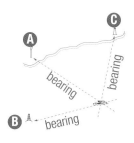

Additional bearings of **B** and **C** are taken to determine the boat's position.

You can use multiple bearings (directions) to fixed objects from your boat to more exactly determine your position and plot it on the chart. In the example shown, bearings **A**, **B** and **C** have been taken from three objects and transferred to the chart. Their intersection (called a *fix*) indicates the boat's position. In actual practice, rarely do all three lines pass through the same precise point. Instead they will form a small triangle. Your position is usually inside the triangle.

Using a Range

Lining up two fixed objects on the same bearing is called a *range*. The objects may be headlands, trees, buildings, towers, beacons, buoys or special range markers. You can use a range to follow a channel, keep in safe water or stay on course.

If you are motoring across a current toward a destination, you need to adjust your course to compensate for the current's effect. You can determine how much to compensate by using a range.

Distance, Speed and Time

The relationship between distance, speed and time can be remembered by:

$$\text{Speed (S)} = \frac{\text{Distance (D) miles}}{\text{Time (T) hour}} \qquad \text{or } S = \frac{60^* \times D \text{ (miles)}}{T \text{ (minutes)}}$$

*60 converts hours to minutes

Speed at sea is measured in knots, which are nautical miles per hour (1 knot = 1.15 mph). While larger boats may have electronic instruments or GPS navigation systems that measure speed and distance, these instruments are not typically found on small powerboats.

Calculating Speed. If you motored distance A (which the dividers measure as 2 nautical miles) in 6 minutes, your speed would be calculated as 20 knots.

$$S = \frac{60 \times D}{T} = \frac{60 \times 2 \text{ nautical miles}}{6 \text{ minutes}} \qquad S = 20 \text{ knots}$$

Calculating Distance. If you have been motoring at 10 knots for 12 minutes, then you have run a distance of 2 miles.

$$D = \frac{S \times T}{60} = \frac{10 \text{ knots} \times 12 \text{ minutes}}{60} \qquad D = 2 \text{ miles}$$

By lining up the two markers of this "official" range, you will be able to stay in the middle of the channel.

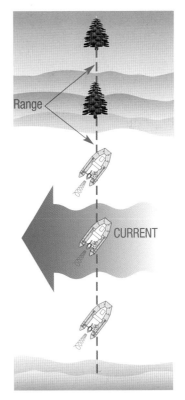

By lining up the two trees of this "natural" range, you will be able to reach your destination in a straight line.

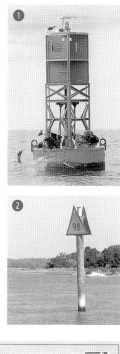

Calculating Time. If you plan to cover distance A while running your boat at 15 knots, then you can estimate that it will take 8 minutes to do it.

$$T = \frac{60 \times D}{S} = \frac{60 \times 2 \text{ nautical miles}}{15 \text{ knots}} \qquad T = 8 \text{ minutes}$$

Aids to Navigation

Navigation aids are nautical road signs that can be used to help you determine your position, follow a safe course and to warn of dangers. Aids to navigation may be divided into two broad categories:

❶ **Buoys** are floating marks anchored (moored) in a fixed position. Buoy positions depicted on a nautical chart are approximate within the swing movement allowed by the scope of their mooring cable. Be aware they can sometimes drag from their position as a result of storms, ice or impact with a ship.

❷ **Beacons** are fixed to the sea bottom or located on shore, making them a reliable and precise aid for navigating. Beacons include daymarks, beacons with topmarks, ranges and lighthouses.

Lighted buoys and beacons can be identified by their color (red, green, white, or yellow) and rhythm (pattern of their flashes). There are a variety of rhythms displayed by various lights. These are identified on charts. NOTE: most unlit marks have reflective tape that will be picked up by your searchlight.

There are three different navigation marking systems used in U.S. waters:

❶ The U.S. Marking system is used on all navigable waters in the U.S., with the exception of the Mississippi River and its tributaries and the Intracoastal Waterway.

❷ The Intracoastal Waterway system

❸ The Western River system used on the Mississippi River and its tributaries.

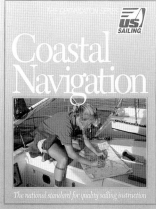

See the Aids to Navigation chapter in the book *Coastal Navigation* for more information on navigation aids*.

* order online at www.uspowerboating.com

U.S. Marking System

Lateral Marks. A system of lateral marks is used to indicate on which side a mark should be passed when returning from seaward. In U.S. waters, red marks are kept on your right (starboard) side and green ones on your left (port) side. Remember this orientation by the "3 Rs" of "RED, RIGHT, RETURNING (from seaward)." When an approach from seaward cannot be determined, the Conventional Direction is used, which is a clockwise rotation around the U.S. land mass and northerly and westerly in the Great Lakes, except for southerly in Lake Michigan.

The Conventional Direction for lateral marks is a clockwise rotation around the U.S.

STARBOARD (RIGHT) LATERAL MARKS
Color: **RED**
Shape: **NUNS OR TRIANGLES**
Character: **EVEN NUMBERS**
Light: **RED** (if lighted)

PORT (LEFT) LATERAL MARKS
Color: **GREEN**
Shape: **CANS** or **SQUARES**
Character: **ODD NUMBERS**
Light: **GREEN** (if lighted)

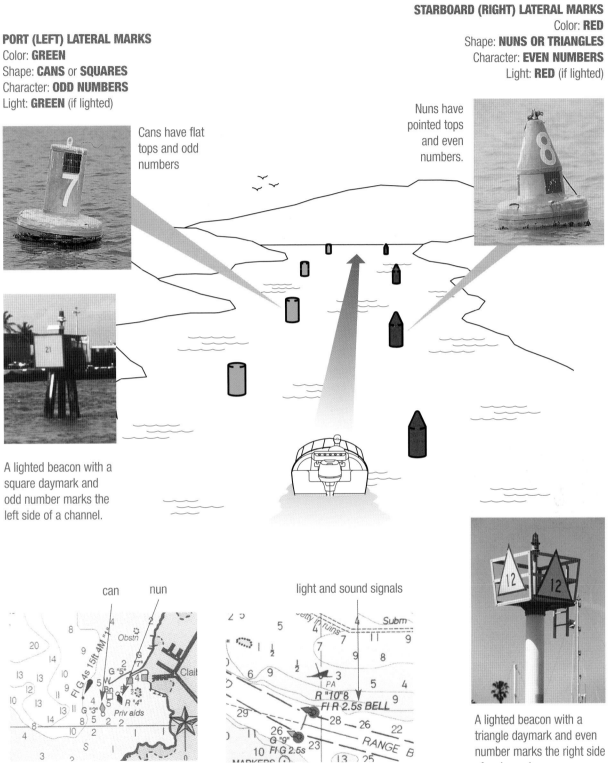

Cans have flat tops and odd numbers

Nuns have pointed tops and even numbers.

A lighted beacon with a square daymark and odd number marks the left side of a channel.

A lighted beacon with a triangle daymark and even number marks the right side of a channel.

can   nun

light and sound signals

Red buoys on the chart have an "R" indicating their color, while greens often do not. Note also the odd number on the green can (G "3") and the even numbers on the red nun (R "4"). If red or green buoy has a light and/or sound signal, this is also noted (Fl R 2.5s BELL).

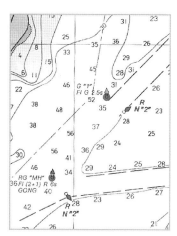

This lighted preferred channel buoy is identified on the chart by RG "MH" Fl (2+1) R 6s. The RG symbol indicates that the top band is red (R), which tells us that the preferred channel is to the left. We can also identify the buoy by the letters "MH" on it.

This is an unlighted preferred channel buoy with green and red horizontal bands and the letters, "NR".

Preferred Channel Marks. When channels divide, one will be "preferred" for deeper draft vessels. It may or may not be the one you want, but at the division you will find a preferred channel buoy. It may be passed on either side but will exhibit a preferred side based on the color of the uppermost band. If the main channel is to your left, when returning from seaward, the top band will be red indicating the buoy is to be passed on your right (starboard) side. If the top band is green that indicates the preferred channel is to the right and the buoy is to be passed on your left (port) side.

Color: red and green horizontal bands

Shape: cans, squares, nuns, and triangles

Character: letter (s)

Light: same color as uppermost band (if lighted) and is a group flashing light, e.g., Gp Fl (2+1) 6s (2 flashes and 1 flash every 6 seconds).

Safe Water Marks. These marks denote navigable (safe) water on all sides of them. They are frequently used to identify the middle of a channel or an offshore approach point to a channel.

Color: red and white vertical stripes

Shape: sphere or buoy with a red spherical topmark

Character: letter (s)

Light: white (if lighted) and flashes the Morse code (Mo) signal for the letter "A" (i.e., 1 short flash followed by 1 long flash)

This lighted safe water buoy at the seaward approach to the Winyah Bay channel is identified by the symbols RW (red and white stripes) and Mo A (light flashes Morse code "A"). "WB" indicates it is the safe water mark for the Winyah Bay entrance.

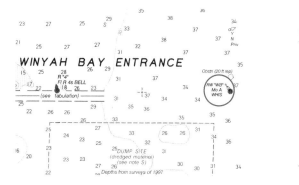

These illustrations show a variety of safe water marks.

Isolated Danger Marks. These are part of the Federal marking system and should not be confused with the state and local danger marks covered below. They are placed near an isolated danger with navigable water all around. They have black and red horizontal bands with a topmark of two black spheres. If lighted, they display a group flashing of two white flashes every 5 seconds.

Special Purpose Marks. These are not navigation marks, but are used to alert you to a special feature or area such as the Triton submarine turning basin at the mouth of the St. Mary's River. They also mark pipelines, traffic separation schemes, spoil areas, and jetties. These marks can be identified by their yellow color with black letter(s). If lighted, they display a yellow fixed or flashing light. You will have to refer to a chart, Notices to Mariners, Coast Pilot or Light List to determine their meaning.

Information and Regulatory Marks. These come under the control of state or local regulatory bodies and are used to alert you to warnings and regulatory matters. They have orange geometric borders displayed against a white background.

Intracoastal Waterway System

Boaters on the East Coast of the United States and the Gulf of Mexico should be aware of the Intracoastal Waterway (ICW), also called "The Ditch." This protected waterway uses its own, unique markings. When following the ICW from New Jersey to Texas, a yellow ▲ should be left to starboard and a yellow ■ to port, *regardless of the color of the navigation aid on which they appear.* The prudent navigator will follow charts closely and carry an up-to-date ICW cruising guide.

Since there is no obvious approach from seaward for the Intracoastal Waterway, the Conventional Direction of clockwise rotation around the U.S. land mass is used. As a result, the marks toward the mainland side of the waterway are designated as marking the right side of the Waterway, and the ones toward the sea are the left side (see below).

The Intracoastal Waterway is a network of protected inland water routes winding from New Jersey to Texas

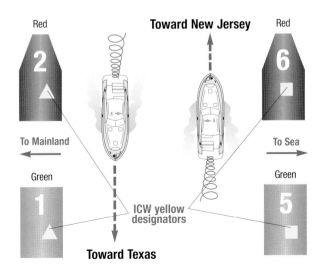

There are places along the ICW where the Waterway and a channel leading in from the sea coincide. If the directions of the two systems are the same, the yellow triangles will be on the red starboard marks and the yellow squares on green port marks. But if the conventional direction of the Waterway system runs opposite to the "returning from seaward" direction of the channel, the U.S. Marking system for the channel prevails and the yellow triangles will be on channel's green marks and the yellow squares on the red marks. Extreme care should be exercised when passing the junction of the Intracoastal Waterway and a channel leading in from the sea. The mixture of marks can be very confusing, but if you follow the yellow ICW symbols, you should not get lost.

The yellow triangle on this red daymark indicates the starboard (mainland) side of the ICW channel.

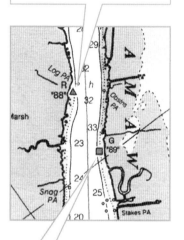

The yellow square on this green daymark marks the port (seaward) side of the ICW channel.

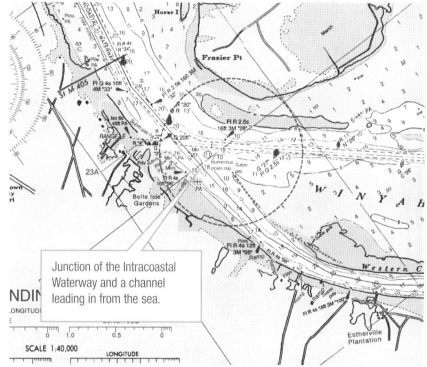

Junction of the Intracoastal Waterway and a channel leading in from the sea.

SCALE 1:40,000

Western River System

This is used on the Mississippi River and its tributaries above Baton Rouge. It is also used on certain other rivers emptying into the Gulf of Mexico. Its major differences from the U.S. Marking system are:
• Aids to navigation are not numbered or lettered. Numbers on marks represent mileages.
• Safe water and isolated danger marks are not used.
• Lights on green aids show a single flashing green or white light.
• Lights on red aids show a red or white group flashing light.
• Diamond-shaped crossing boards indicate where the channel crosses from one riverbank to the other.

Bridge Markings

Bridges that can be opened are marked as follows:
• Red lights mark a closed bridge and the piers of the bridge.
• Green lights mark a bridge when it is open.
• A green light also marks the centerline of a passage through the bridge.
• If more than one passage exists, the preferred channel is marked with three vertical white lights in addition to the green light.
• Centerlines of channels through bridges may also be marked with conventional red and green lights, but in that case the piers are marked with fixed yellow lights.

REVIEW QUESTIONS

1. On a Mercator chart one minute (1') of latitude is equal to _____ nautical mile(s).
2. The error to a compass reading that is created by objects on your boat with magnetic properties is called _____.
   a. compass card
   b. deviation
   c. variation
3. Our estimated boat speed is 8 knots (nautical miles per hour). In 30 minutes the boat will have traveled _____ nautical miles.
4. When returning from seaward red marks are kept to the _____ side of the boat.
5. Marks of the Intracoastal Waterway System are differentiated from normal lateral system marks by a _____ (color) triangle or square on the mark.

13. Health, Safety & Emergencies

KEY CONCEPTS

▶ Hypothermia & heat emergencies   ▶ Emergencies
▶ Hazards   ▶ Disabled boat

It is good seamanship to be prepared and able to deal with any emergency, should it occur.

Hypothermia & Heat Emergencies

Hypothermia. Hypothermia occurs when the body temperature drops below normal. Prolonged exposure to cool air and/or cool spray or precipitation can cause hypothermia. Dress properly to prevent this from happening. Immersion in water accelerates loss of body heat. As water temperature decreases, it becomes increasingly important to get a victim out of the water as quickly as possible. After an hour in water of 32 degrees Fahrenheit, there is a high probability of death; after more than an hour in 50-degree water, the victim is in the danger zone.

Heat Emergencies. Heat emergencies can also be life threatening. High temperature and humidity are the usual culprits. Be alert for signals whenever the temperature is around 90 degrees Fahrenheit and the relative humidity is more than 70%. Young children and elderly people are particularly vulnerable. The best preventive measure is to avoid dehydration by drinking plenty of water at regular intervals. It also helps to dress in cool clothing (see Chapter 4) and stay in the shade of a boat's awning as much as possible.

Seasickness

Seasickness occurs when your body tries to adjust to the change in motion on a boat. You may be uncomfortable at first, but most people get their "sea legs" after a short time. Early symptoms include yawning, drowsiness, slight sweating or cooling of the skin. More advanced symptoms are burping, nausea, and vomiting. React as early as possible by getting on deck, breathing fresh air, focusing on the horizon and helping your body to actively adjust to the wave motion. Avoid cooking, reading, or navigating.

Various treatments are available. Scopolamine ear patches release medication over time. Some people find wrist pressure bands helpful. Avoid alcohol, eat moderately, and replace lost nutrients and liquids. You may also find relief by wedging yourself into a bunk with pillows and sleeping.

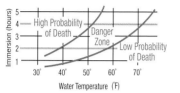

The danger of hypothermia increases as water temperature declines and the duration of immersion increases.

Chart courtesy USCG Office of Boating Safety

HYPOTHERMIA

SIGNALS...
▶ Shivering
▶ Impaired judgment
▶ Dizziness
▶ Numbness
▶ Change in level of consciousness
▶ Weakness
▶ Glassy stare
(Physical symptoms may vary, since age, body size, and clothing will cause individual differences.)

TREATMENT...
Medical assistance should be given to anyone with hypothermia. Until medical assistance arrives, these steps should be taken:
▶ Check breathing and pulse.
▶ Gently move the person to a warm place.
▶ Carefully remove all wet clothing. Gradually warm person by wrapping in blankets or putting on dry clothes. Do not warm person too quickly, such as immersing in warm water. Rapid rewarming may cause dangerous heart rhythms. Hot water bottles and chemical heat packs may be used if wrapped in a towel or blanket before applying.
▶ Give warm, nonalcoholic and decaffeinated liquids to a conscious person only.

HEAT EXHAUSTION

SIGNALS...
▶ Cool, moist, pale skin
▶ Heavy sweating
▶ Headache
▶ Dizziness
▶ Nausea
▶ Weakness, exhaustion

TREATMENT...
Without prompt care, heat exhaustion can advance to a more serious condition — heat stroke. First aid includes:
▶ Move person to cool environment.
▶ Remove clothing soaked with perspiration and loosen any tight clothing.
▶ Apply cool, wet towels or sheets.
▶ Fan the person.
▶ Give person a half glass (4 oz.) of cool water every 15 min.

HEAT STROKE

SIGNALS...
▶ Red, hot, dry or moist skin
▶ Very high skin temperature
▶ Changes in level of consciousness
▶ Vomiting
▶ Rapid, weak pulse
▶ Rapid, shallow breathing

TREATMENT...
Heat stroke is life threatening. Anyone suffering from heat stroke needs to be cooled and an EMS technician should be contacted immediately. To care for heat stroke:
▶ Move person to cool environment.
▶ Apply cool, wet towels or sheets.
▶ If available, place ice or cold packs on the person's wrists and ankles, groin, each armpit, and neck.
▶ If unconscious, check breathing and pulse.

NOTE: First Aid and CPR classes are available nationwide. It is recommended that you attend one.

Electrical Hazards

When using electrical power tools near water or stringing extension cords along docks, make sure they are properly grounded and the power cords and connections do not make contact with the water. Overhead power lines can be a dangerous hazard. If they are touched by a long antenna, fishing rod, or some other tall metal object on your boat, the result could be shock or even electrocution. Look upward

Action Plan for Electrical Injury
* *Never approach a victim of an electrical injury until you are sure the power is turned off.*
* *If a power line is down, wait for the fire department and/or power company.*
* *Contact a doctor or EMS personnel immediately.*
* *The victim may have breathing difficulties or be in cardiac arrest. Provide care for any life threatening conditions.*

for power lines in boat launching sites or over water where they could be low-lying. Another potential electrical hazard is snagging your anchor on underwater electrical cables. Check for cable markings on shore or cable location symbols on your chart before anchoring.

Dams

Dams can present a very confusing and often misleading appearance to the boater. Many larger dams incorporate hydroelectric generating plants, road crossings, and in some cases, bypass locks that allow boats to travel around the dam. These large dams are usually well marked and quite obvious. Other dams are not so obvious. Dams that allow the water to flow out of the bottom can trap an unsuspecting boat against the wall by the strong downward flow of the water.

Backflow from a low-head dam can hold a boat against the face of the dam and capsize it.

Low-head dams are designed to maintain a minimum water level upstream. To the unsuspecting boater upstream of the dam, the water flowing over the dam cannot be seen, but if a boat tries to pass over the dam it can be held against the face of the dam and capsize. In some cases the force of the water may be enough to pull a person in a PFD underwater.

Capsizing & Swamping

Most capsizes occur from improper loading with too much weight or improper weight distribution. Ensure that the maximum loading on the boat's maximum capacities label is not exceeded and that the boat is loaded evenly fore and aft and from side to side. If a boat does not have a capacities label, a rule of thumb is maximum number of people equals length of boat times its width divided by 15. It is equally important not to overpower a boat with too large an engine.

Powerboats that have powerful outboards or stern drives will roll significantly if turned too sharply with a sudden burst of power at slow speeds. On smaller boats, this rolling action can be enough to swamp or even capsize them. It may be necessary to reduce power before the outboard can be centered.

Should a capsize occur the cardinal rule is to, "Stay with the boat; don't swim for shore." An overturned boat is much more easily sighted than a swimmer. Everyone should be wearing a PFD. Be aware that a person in the water under duress weakens very quickly. Even in so-called "warm" water, the effects of hypothermia can occur rapidly. Sudden immersion in cold water can lead to sudden cold-water shock reflex, which causes the victim to gasp for air and possibly inhale water. Once in the water, rapid uncontrolled breathing, cardiac arrest and other life threatening situations can also occur. If shivering starts to occur, it is important to reduce heat loss by using the HELP (Heat Escape Lessening Position) position with arms close to the body and knees to the chest, or huddle close together with others in the water. Wearing a PFD will also help reduce heat loss. Any movement will increase the loss.

HELP position minimizes heat loss when submerged in water.

Overboard Prevention

Next to capsizing, falling overboard is the second leading cause of fatal boating accidents. It is also one of the most preventable. Many overboard situations occur before the boat even leaves the dock. Typically, these situations occur when passengers attempt to step aboard while carrying items and slip, or they step on the edge of the boat and lose their balance when the boat tips. Overboard incidents can also happen when people stand up or ride on the boat's bow, gunwales (outer edges) or seatbacks, or are thrown off balance by a careless driver making erratic or sudden changes in speed or direction. To help prevent falling overboard, use footwear with good traction and follow the maxim, "One hand for the boat and one hand for yourself."

Person-In-Water Recovery

Recovery Procedure. Recovering a person in the water (PIW) is a four-stage procedure: 1) make physical contact with PIW, 2) attach PIW to boat, 3) get PIW back aboard, and 4) aftercare.

❶ Make physical contact with PIW:
• If a person falls overboard, immediately swing stern and propeller away from PIW. Shout "Crew Overboard!" and throw buoyant objects such as cushions and life rings toward the PIW as soon as possible. Even if these objects do not come to the aid of the PIW,

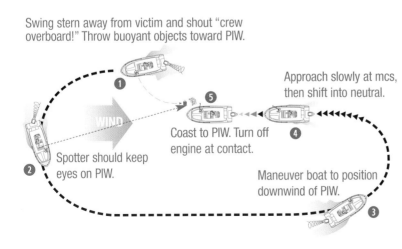

Swing stern away from victim and shout "crew overboard!" Throw buoyant objects toward PIW.

WIND

Spotter should keep eyes on PIW.

Coast to PIW. Turn off engine at contact.

Maneuver boat to position downwind of PIW.

Approach slowly at mcs, then shift into neutral.

they will "litter the water" where he or she went overboard and help your spotter to keep the PIW in sight.

• Designate someone to spot and point to the PIW in the water. The spotter should NEVER take his or her eyes off the PIW.

• Maneuver the boat to a position downwind of the PIW, staying close enough to the PIW to keep him or her in sight while allowing sufficient room to complete the maneuver.

• Approach slowly using intermittent power, bow first, pointing into wind and waves with the PIW on the driver's side. This allows better visibility for the driver, and helps to keep the propeller away from the PIW. Communicate with and reassure the PIW.

• Shift into neutral and coast to PIW, making physical contact with a paddle, boat hook or line. Turn off the engine once reliable contact has been made or if there is any risk of the PIW coming close to the propeller. Keep reassuring the PIW.

❷ **Attach PIW to boat:** Pass a Lifesling (if available) or a looped line around the PIW and attach it to the boat. This will ensure that you don't lose the PIW if he or she weakens and cannot hold on any longer. If the PIW is wearing a safety harness, attach the safety line to the harness and secure to the boat.

❸ **Get PIW back aboard:** This can be the most difficult part of the process. An increasing number of boats have a swimming platform and/or ladder on the transom. If your boat doesn't have one, carry a portable ladder. Some people use the stern drive or cavitation plate as a step, but there is a risk of slipping and getting cut by the propeller. Also if the PIW needs help the engine may be an obstacle. On large powerboats with high sides, a rope sling can be rigged to a davit or pad eye on the side of the cabin. If there are any problems getting the PIW aboard and there is a grave and imminent threat to his or her life, make a "MAYDAY" distress call to the Coast Guard on Channel 16 of your VHF radio or a 911 call on your cellular phone (if within response area of 911).

❹ **Aftercare:** Take the greatest care of rescued PIW who often will be suffering from varying degrees of hypothermia. Refer to the beginning of this chapter for suggested treatment.

Recovery Procedure Using a Lifesling

• If a person falls overboard, immediately swing stern and propeller away from PIW. Shout "Crew Overboard!" and throw buoyant objects such as cushions and life rings toward the PIW as soon as possible.

• Deploy the Lifesling by opening the bag and dropping the sling into the water. It will trail out behind and draw out the remaining line.

The Lifesling is a floating collar attached to the boat by a length of floating line that doubles as a hoisting sling to retrieve a PIW in the water.

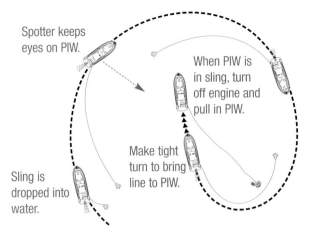

Spotter keeps eyes on PIW.

When PIW is in sling, turn off engine and pull in PIW.

Make tight turn to bring line to PIW.

Sling is dropped into water.

- Circle the boat around the PIW with the line and sling trailing astern (similar to circling a towline to a waterskier in the water). Take care not to run over the floating line.
- Contact is made with the PIW by the line and sling being drawn inward by the boat's circling motion. The PIW then places the sling over head and under arms, and fastens the snap.
- Upon contact, shift into neutral. Once the PIW is in the Lifesling, *stop* the engine and pull the PIW close to the boat.
- Set up boarding equipment and bring PIW aboard the boat (refer to ❸ and ❹ on previous page).

Disabled Boat

Engine Failure. When a boat suddenly loses power and starts drifting, consider whether or not it is in danger. Quickly determine if it is drifting toward rocks, shallow waters or a heavy-traffic shipping channel.
• If there is no danger and you're drifting in safe waters, the best alternative may be to try to fix the problem or call the local towboat rescue service.
• If the water is shallow enough for anchoring, this could be the best alternative until help arrives. Being anchored in a fixed place will also make it easier for the towing service to find you.
• If land is nearby or the wind is favorable, another alternative may be to paddle the boat or even rig a sail from the boat's canopy. Remember, it is always safer to stay with the boat and not attempt to swim for help.

If you cannot fix the problem, you can call the local towing service on the VHF radio channel it monitors or via a cellular phone. You can also use the appropriate distress signals on board your boat to attract the attention of another boat (see Chapter 8). You should not make a

Action Plan for Flooding

If flooding occurs, make sure everyone is wearing a PFD and follow these three steps:

1. *Start pumping and bailing with large solid bucket.*
2. *Locate leak.*
3. *Stop the flow. You may be able to raise the damaged area above the waterline by shifting equipment and people. Pack a hole with some sort of plugging material, such as a shirt, extra life jackets, cushions or even a nerf ball. This temporary remedy may slow the water flow enough to slowly head for a near shore where the boat can be beached.*

If you cannot stem the flooding, this is the time to use your distress signals and call the Coast Guard on Channel 16 of your VHF radio.

Action Plan for Running Aground

- *Check crew for possible injury.*
- *Determine damage to boat.*
- *Attempt to free boat without causing further damage.*

"MAYDAY" distress call to the U.S. Coast Guard unless there is a grave and imminent (actually happening) danger to the vessel or the life of a person(s) on board.

Flooding. If a boat is taking on water, it could be caused by damage to the hull from hitting an underwater object or crashing off waves at high speeds. Many outboard-driven powerboats have double hulls. If the operator suspects an impact was hard enough to damage the outer hull, every effort should be made to determine whether the space between the hulls is flooding. Another possibility is failure of a through-hull fitting, such as a seacock. An inboard engine offers additional possibilities, such as a broken hose line in its cooling system, a torn outdrive boot or a leaking seal at the stern tube on a "fixed" propeller drive system.

Running Aground. The severity of this situation depends on how fast the boat was moving and the hardness of the ground. The combination of high speed and a hard, rocky bottom can cause extensive damage to the hull, as well as serious injury to occupants. Slow and soft impact is most likely an uneventful self-rescue situation. After running aground, make a full damage assessment and check for leaks before freeing the boat. If the boat is holed you may not want to float free until you've stopped the flow of water.

Generally, when boats with outboards or stern drives hit bottom, the skeg and propeller will be the first to strike. If the neoprene hub (or shear pin) is still intact, you may be able to free the boat by quickly reducing the throttle to idle rpm and then shifting into neutral. Next tilt the outboard motor into the shallow water position and try to carefully back off in the direction you came from. Strong backing thrust from the propeller may pile sand up, blocking the hull from moving backward. Another alternative is to move everyone forward to raise the stern and push the boat off with a paddle. If the neoprene hub is damaged, you'll be able to run the outboard, but only at low power.

❶ Reduce throttle to idle rpm and shift into neutral.

❷ Tilt outboard to shallow water position and shift into reverse to back off.

Skeg hits soft bottom

If the boat is firmly stuck and the tide is rising, the best course may be to get an anchor out in the direction of deep water and keep a strain on it, and wait while the tide floats the boat off.

An anchor can also be used to help pull your boat free (*kedge off*). It can be placed in position by carrying it out in a small inflatable boat, or floating it with cushions or extra PFDs and swimming it out. Keep a strain on it the whole time you are attempting to free the boat. When the boat breaks free, take up on the line and keep it clear of the propeller.

If you cannot get off, you'll need the assistance of a professional towboat rescue service. If another boater offers to help, use great caution. Lines used to pull a grounded boat clear are put under tremendous strain as well as the chocks and cleats. Cleats on small pleasure boats frequently cannot withstand such loads. If a line should break or a cleat pulls away, injury can result.

Fire. Nothing can be more frightening than the sudden outbreak of a fire on board. The importance of strategically placed and fully charged fire extinguishers cannot be overly stressed (see Chapter 8 for fire extinguishers requirements). The most effective way of preventing a fire is ensuring that fuel and gear are stowed properly and that bilges are kept clean.

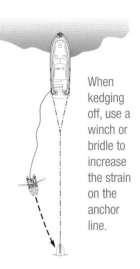

When kedging off, use a winch or bridle to increase the strain on the anchor line.

Action Plan for Fire

- *The first person to see a fire should shout "Fire!" and everyone should move on deck wearing a PFD.*
- *Steer the boat so as to lessen any wind and to keep the smoke clear of people on board.*
- *If danger seems imminent and life-threatening, use your distress signals and make a "MAYDAY" distress call to the Coast Guard on Channe16 of your VHF radio or a 911 call on your cellular phone (if within response area of 911).*
- *Prepare to abandon the boat.*

Types of fires	Extinguishing methods
CLASS A: wood, paper, cloth, rubber, some plastics	① Water, poured or hosed, on flames ② Dry chemical extinguisher ③ Fire blanket for contained galley fires ④ FE-241, FM-200 automatic extinguishers (Halon replacements)
Class B: flammable liquids including diesel, oil, gasoline, alcohol	① Dry chemical extinguisher ② Carbon dioxide (CO_2) extinguisher ③ FE-241, FM-200 automatic extinguishers
Class C: live electrical fires	① Carbon dioxide (CO_2) extinguisher ② Dry chemical extinguisher ③ FE-241, FM-200 automatic extinguishers

Most fires can be controlled providing the boater acts immediately and properly. Know how to use your extinguisher and take the opportunity to practice its use. When using an extinguisher, sweep its discharge across the base of the fire and keep going until the extinguisher is empty. Watch the remnants for re-ignition. An easy way to remember proper procedure in an emergency situation is the acronym PASS: **P**ull pin, **A**im at fire base, **S**queeze handle, **S**weep side to side using short bursts.

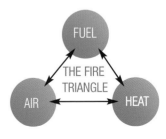

Some form of fuel, heat and air are the three elements necessary for fire to occur.

Towing and Being Towed

There are professional towboat rescue services in many areas that will respond to your request for a tow. They can be reached by VHF radio or cellular phone. Keep their telephone numbers on board your boat in case you need to call them. If you ever need a tow or have to help another boat in trouble, consider the following:

- A towline of 100 feet of 1/2-inch or 5/8-inch double braided nylon is suggested. If an anchor line is used, make sure it is in good condition. If nylon line breaks under load, it has a dangerous whipping action.
- If there is no towing eye, rig a bridle (see detail) to split the load. If the reliability of the cleats or eyes are questionable, it may be necessary to wrap the towline completely around the boat.
- Do not stand near or in line with the towline and bridle, in case it breaks or cleats pull out.
- Everyone should wear a PFD.

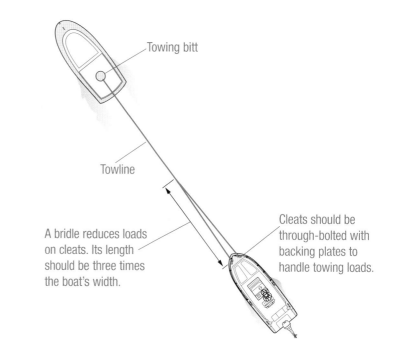

Towing bitt

Towline

A bridle reduces loads on cleats. Its length should be three times the boat's width.

Cleats should be through-bolted with backing plates to handle towing loads.

Towing Tips
- *Operator of towboat briefs boat to be towed and a means of communication (i.e., hand signals or VHF radio) is established.*
- *Start the tow slowly, maintaining a steady strain on the towline, and tow at a moderate, safe speed.*
- *Adjust the length of the towline so that both boats climb up and slide down waves at the same time.*
- *Make wide turns.*

- *Avoid bow-down trim to maintain steering control.*
- *On the boat being towed, raise the outboard motor to the "up" position and lock it. If the boat weaves out of control, you may have to lower motor to help it track, which will require a much slower towing speed.*
- *Steer towed boat with rudder to follow behind towboat.*
- *Allow plenty of time for the tow to slow down before attempting to release the tow.*
- *Be prepared to shorten up on the towline when entering an anchorage.*
- *Tow to the nearest safe anchorage, harbor or marina.*

REVIEW QUESTIONS

1. If your boat capsizes, you should _____ the boat.
   a. leave
   b. recover
   c. anchor
   d. stay with
2. To recover a person from the water it is best to approach from _____ of the person.
3. If your boat experiences engine failure and you are not in grave and imminent danger you should _____.
   a. swim to shore
   b. tie onto a channel buoy
   c. stay with the boat
   d. make a Mayday call
4. When using a fire extinguisher, sweep the discharge across the _____ of the fire.
5. To extinguish a diesel or gasoline fire, you should use _____.
   a. water
   b. a fire blanket
   c. a wet chemical extinguisher
   d. a dry chemical extinguisher

Answers: 1) d. stay with 2) downwind 3) c. stay with the boat 4) base 5) d. a dry chemical extinguisher

14. Launching & Trailering

KEY CONCEPTS
▶ Trailering considerations   ▶ Using hoists
▶ Using a ramp

A boat on a trailer expands the range of boating opportunities, and your ability to easily use a ramp or hoist will add to the enjoyment of your on-water experience. Preparation and a little maneuvering practice with your vehicle and trailer are the keys to success.

Trailering

The combined weight of boat and trailer affects the vehicle in several ways:
❶ its ability to pull and stop;
❷ the weight on the hitch may depress the vehicle's rear suspension to the point where the front wheels become light on the road, making it difficult to steer and blinding oncoming drivers with high headlights;
❸ additional wear on brakes, transmission, suspension and tires as well as possible engine overheating.
Check the owner's manual (or contact a dealer) for manufacturer's limits, warranty requirements and suggested packages for towing.

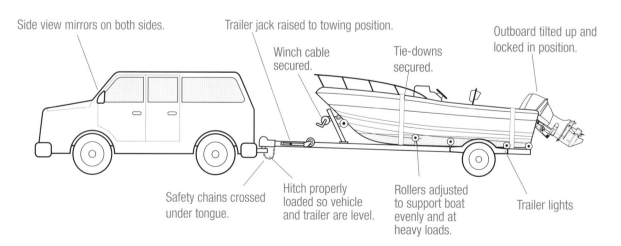

Side view mirrors on both sides.

Trailer jack raised to towing position.

Winch cable secured.

Tie-downs secured.

Outboard tilted up and locked in position.

Safety chains crossed under tongue.

Hitch properly loaded so vehicle and trailer are level.

Rollers adjusted to support boat evenly and at heavy loads.

Trailer lights

Trailer Inspection

Trailer hitches. Conventional hitches come in five classifications (I, II, III, IV, V) that are rated for different gross trailer weights and tongue weights. Avoid hitches attached to bumpers. The weight on a hitch ball (tongue weight) typically ranges from 5% to 10% of the combined weight of the trailer and boat with fuel and gear. If the tongue weight is too light, the trailer can swerve back and forth ("fishtail") on the road. If it's too heavy, the vehicle will be difficult to steer.

Safety Chains. Safety chains should be used and crossed under the tongue and attached to the vehicle's frame. They should not drag on the ground or come under tension when making a tight turn.

Tires & Brakes. Tires (including spare) should be inflated to recommended pressure and trailer brakes checked to insure they are working properly. Brakes are activated either electrically or with a surge hydraulic system. Each type has its pros and cons. Check your state law and talk with experienced boaters in your area to determine what type best meets your needs. Many states require trailer brakes when the combined weight of the trailer and boat exceeds 3,000 lbs, but the limit can go as low as 1,500 lbs.

Wheel Bearings. Check wheel bearings for signs of wear (each side of the hub has a bearing). Signs of worn bearings are: noise as wheel rotates, wheel wobble, smoke or excessive heat at the hub, or grease residue sprayed on wheel or boat. Bearings should be removed and checked every 1,000 miles or at the beginning of each season. Waterproof bearings and/or spring-loaded bearing protector caps are recommended. Lubricate the bearings with marine-grade waterproof grease, being careful not to use too much.

Boat Support. Be sure roller supports or bunks (pads) support boat evenly along centerline, near chine and at transom, and at locations where weight is concentrated. Secure gear to prevent movement and lock outboard or stern drive in towing position. Make sure tie-downs are snug and secured. Drain plugs should be removed and stowed.

Driving Tips While Trailering
- *Allow extra time and space to accelerate and stop.*
- *When slowing down or stopping, gradually increase pressure on trailer and car brakes. Avoid hitting the brakes hard. This is especially dangerous on wet roads and could jackknife the trailer. Sudden stops while turning may also jackknife the trailer.*
- *If the trailer starts to fishtail, minimize steering and slowly reduce speed until the fishtailing stops.*
- *When driving downhill, shift into lower gear to avoid excessive brake wear.*
- *When turning, make a wider turning radius to prevent the trailer from hitting an obstacle on the inside of your turn. Use the rear-view mirror to check trailer clearance to the obstacle.*
- *In windy or truck-passing conditions, trailers may have a tendency to fishtail. Tow at a slower speed in these conditions.*

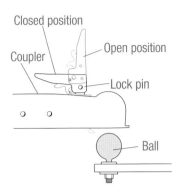

Ball should match coupler size and should be lightly greased. There are three ball sizes: 1 7/8 inches (typically rated for 2,000 pounds), 2 inches (rated anywhere from 3,500 pounds to 6,000 pounds), and 2 5/16 inches (6,000 to 10,000 pounds). The coupler usually has the ball size marked on it along with the maximum gross weight and maximum tongue weight (combined weight of the trailer and boat on the ball).

Spare Parts List
- Spare trailer bearings, seals and grease
- Spare trailer tire
- Spare bulbs for trailer lights
- Trailer jack and lug wrench
- Spare tie-downs and lines

- *Reduce speed for bumps or depressions in the road.*
- *When backing a trailer, avoid over-steering. Turn the bottom of the steering wheel in the direction you want the back of the trailer to turn.*
- *Some states have lower speed limits for trailering.*
- *Check the trailer, boat and tie-downs periodically.*

Launching

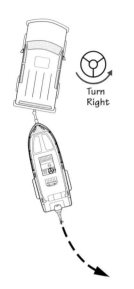

When backing a trailer, turn the bottom of the steering wheel in the direction you want the trailer to turn.

❶ Get the boat ready to launch in an area that does not block the ramp. Insert and secure drain plugs, remove tie-downs (except for winch cable), unplug wiring connector, add boat gear, attach bow and stern lines, connect fuel line attachments, and complete starting checks. Allow the trailer's wheel bearings and lights to cool before launching to avoid damaging them by sudden cooling.

❷ Back trailer slowly down ramp until boat is in water. Use rear-view mirrors to keep both sides of ramp in view when backing. Know where the end of the ramp stops to avoid running the trailer's wheels off it. Many ramps have a mark to indicate its end. Avoid immersing the vehicle's exhaust pipes in the water. A tongue extension may be required to launch deeper draft boats or for shallow slope ramps.

❸ Park in first or "park" gear and place a block behind the vehicle's rear wheel.

❹ Have someone take the bow line so the boat won't float away.

❺ Detach the winch cable from the boat.

❻ Start the boat and back away.

❼ Remove the vehicle and trailer from the ramp as soon as possible.

CAUTION: Be aware of slippery ramps. They can cause injury or make it difficult for vehicles with or without four-wheel drive to pull a boat up the ramp. Before launching, open a window in case the vehicle accidentally slips off the ramp and becomes submerged.

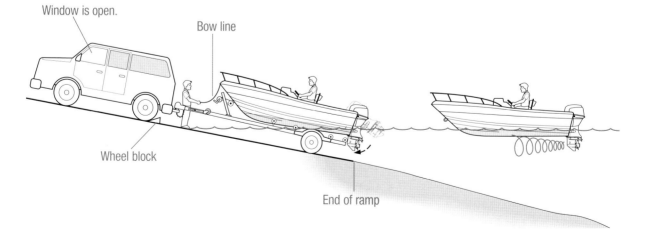

Window is open.

Bow line

Wheel block

End of ramp

Hauling Out

❶ Back trailer down ramp until about two-thirds of the rollers/bunks are in the water. Park in first or "park" gear and block rear wheel.

❷ Approach trailer slowly, lining up the centerline of the boat with the centerline of the trailer, shift into neutral to let boat float on trailer. Some people prefer to use the engine to get on the trailer, called "power loading," but be aware that some ramp facilities may prohibit this method.

❸ Attach winch cable to boat eye and take up cable until bow is snug against stop. Lock cable. Be sure to operate the winch while standing to one side to avoid getting hit if the cable breaks.

❹ Check that the center of the transom is over centerline of trailer if there are no trailer side posts or guide rails. If the transom is off centerline, try shifting into forward gear at the throttle's "idle" setting and turn outboard to swing transom over centerline. Do not advance throttle.

❺ Raise outboard or stern drive into towing position and lock.

❻ Pull trailer up ramp at slow, steady speed.

❼ Clear the ramp area.

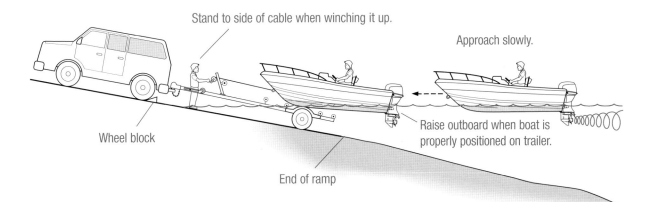

Stand to side of cable when winching it up.

Approach slowly.

Raise outboard when boat is properly positioned on trailer.

Wheel block

End of ramp

Washing Boat and Trailer

There is an increasing problem with boats and trailers picking up aquatic nuisance species (e.g., zebra mussels) from one body of water and introducing them to other waters or lakes. Away from the ramp and run-off areas, remove the drain plugs and wash down the trailer, boat and boat's gear with high water pressure. Flush the cooling system of outboards with a flusher attachment to the water hose. Remove contents of live wells and bait buckets on land.

Hoist Operation

If a hoist is not operated properly, it can result in serious damage and injury. Some facilities require specific personnel to operate the hoist. If you are not at such a facility and haven't operated the hoist before, ask an experienced person to demonstrate or help. Operate the hoist carefully and don't rush. Often safety rules will be posted. Be sure to review them carefully beforehand.

Hoist Preparation

- Drain any water from the boat and close the drain plugs securely.
- Check the condition of the lifting slings, their fittings, and the attachment points on the boat. Their breaking strength should be at least twice the weight of the boat fully loaded, including fuel and gear.
- Slings are fitted so the boat is level when on the hoist.
- Slings are securely fastened.
- Bow and stern lines are attached to boat.
- Outboard or stern drive is locked in the towing position.

REVIEW QUESTIONS

1. The weight on a hitch ball is known as _____.
2. If the tongue weight is too light, a trailer may swerve back and forth, or _____. If this occurs, _____ speed.
3. When backing a trailer, move the _____ of the wheel in the direction you want the back of the trailer to turn.
4. When launching, once the boat is in the water, park in first gear or "park" and place a _____ behind the vehicle's rear wheel.
5. To avoid introducing nuisance species from one body of water to another, it is important to _____ the trailer, boat and boat's gear after hauling out.

Answers: 1) tongue weight 2) fishtail; reduce 3) bottom 4) block 5) wash down / wash

Additional Resources

Online Resources

Directory of State Boating Law Administrators:
http://www.nasbla.org/blas.htm

National Ocean Service home page:
http://www.nos.noaa.gov/

Tidal predictions: http://co-ops.nos.noaa.gov/tp4days.html

Tidal current predictions at U.S. reference stations:
http://co-ops.nos.noaa.gov/refcurrents.html

Tidal current predictions:
http://www.co-ops.nos.noaa.gov/currpred.html

National Weather Service (NWS) home page:
http://www.nws.noaa.gov/

Local weather information: http://www.srh.noaa.gov/

Marine forecast offices:
http://www.nws.noaa.gov/om/marine/marine_map.htm

Powerboat Training: http://www.uspowerboating.com/

U.S. Coast Guard home page:
http://www.uscg.mil/USCG.shtm

Local Notices to Mariners:
http://www.navcen.uscg.gov/lnm/

Office of Boating Safety: http://www.uscgboating.org/

U.S. Environmental Protection Agency home page:
http://www.epa.gov/

Location of no-discharge zones:
http://www.epa.gov/owow/oceans/regulatory/
vessel_sewage/vsdnozone.html

U.S. Sailing Association's Training Office:
http://www.ussailing.org/training/

Publications

Safety, Rescue & Support Boat
Covers must-read information for boat operators involved in safety, rescue and race support operations.

Coastal Navigation
A presentation of charts and illustrations that makes navigating and piloting easy to understand and apply.

Passage Making
Covers a wide range of topics for coastal and offshore passage makers.

Powerboat Certification Standards
Details the standards for each of the certification levels.

Official Logbook
A useful logbook for recording boating, cruising and chartering experiences.

Any of these publications (above) can be ordered on the Powerboat Training website www.uspowerboating.com/

Navigation Rules, International-Inland
Contains all the Navigation Rules discussed in Chapter 11 plus more. It can be downloaded from
http://www.uscg.mil/vtm/navrules/navrules.pdf or ordered from the U.S. Govt. Printing Office at
http://bookstore.gpo.gov/

Also...

Boatowner's Mechanical & Electrical Manual,
by Nigel Calder, International Marine 1996

Reed's Nautical Almanac, annual

Summary of Basic Aids to Navigation

Lateral Aids to Navigation

Lateral marks (below) indicate channels, safe water (mid-channel), and preferred channels (junction buoys) as well as the side on which to leave them when returning to port.

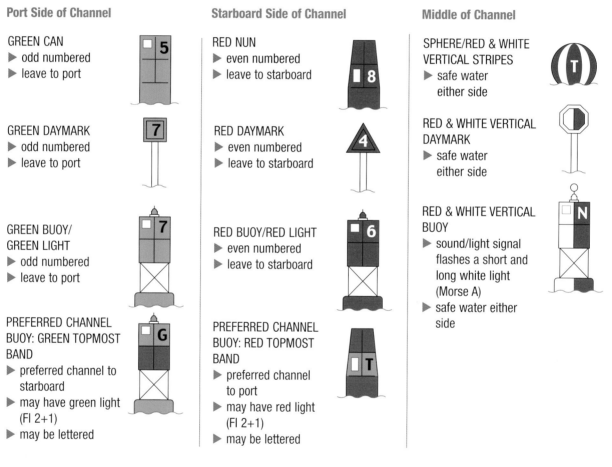

Port Side of Channel

GREEN CAN
- odd numbered
- leave to port

GREEN DAYMARK
- odd numbered
- leave to port

GREEN BUOY/ GREEN LIGHT
- odd numbered
- leave to port

PREFERRED CHANNEL BUOY: GREEN TOPMOST BAND
- preferred channel to starboard
- may have green light (Fl 2+1)
- may be lettered

Starboard Side of Channel

RED NUN
- even numbered
- leave to starboard

RED DAYMARK
- even numbered
- leave to starboard

RED BUOY/RED LIGHT
- even numbered
- leave to starboard

PREFERRED CHANNEL BUOY: RED TOPMOST BAND
- preferred channel to port
- may have red light (Fl 2+1)
- may be lettered

Middle of Channel

SPHERE/RED & WHITE VERTICAL STRIPES
- safe water either side

RED & WHITE VERTICAL DAYMARK
- safe water either side

RED & WHITE VERTICAL BUOY
- sound/light signal flashes a short and long white light (Morse A)
- safe water either side

Information and Regulatory Marks

These marks are used for warnings or regulatory matters.

BOAT EXCLUSION AREA

SWIM / AREA

Explanation may be placed outside the crossed diamond shape, such as dam, rapids, swim area, etc.

DANGER

ROCK

The nature of danger may be indicated inside the diamond shape, such as rock, wreck, shoal, dam, etc.

CONTROLLED AREA

SLOW

NO   WAKE

Type of control is indicated in the circle, such as slow, no wake, anchoring, etc.

Lighthouses

Lighthouses fall into the category of lighted beacons and are fixed to the sea bottom or on land. Charts indicate a lighthouse with a magenta symbol (looks like an exclamation point) and identify the characteristic flashing sequence of its light (e.g., flashing, occulting, group flashing or isophase). Examples: Fl 15s indicates light flashes once every 15 seconds; Fl(2) 5s indicates a Group Flash 2 every 5 seconds.

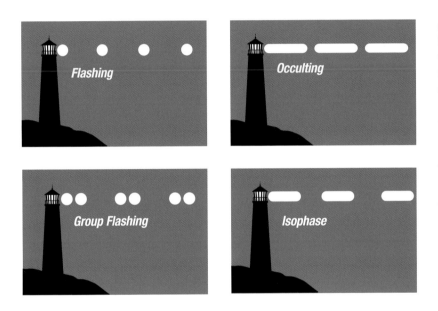

A **flashing** light is on in short bursts interspersed with longer periods of darkness. A **group flashing** light repeats multiple light signals. A **composite flashing** light repeats irregular multiples of signals, or example "2+1". This means that within its time cycle the light will flash a group of 2 flashes followed by a short pause, then a third flash.

An **occulting** light is on most of the time and "winks" off according to its charted sequence. Sometimes called a "black flash," these lights are easy to take bearings on. An **isophase** light has equal periods of light and darkness.

Intracoastal Waterway System

When following the Intracoastal Waterway System (ICW) from New Jersey to Texas, a yellow ▲ should be left to starboard and a yellow ■ to port, *regardless of the color of the navigation aid on which they appear.*

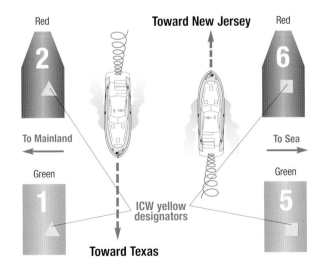

Summary of Basic Sound Signals and Navigation Lights

Sound Signals

• A short blast is about one second's duration.

— A prolonged blast is from four to six seconds' duration.

For vessels in sight of each other:

• One short blast indicates *altering* course to starboard (International), or *intending* to alter course to starboard (Inland) when meeting or crossing.

•• Two short blasts indicate *altering* course to port (International), or *intending* to alter course to port (Inland) when meeting or crossing.

••• Three short blasts indicate engine is in reverse (although vessel may still be moving forward).

••••• Five short blasts = danger.

For vessels in restricted visibility:

— One prolonged blast every two minutes indicates a vessel under power.

— •• One prolonged blast followed by two short blasts every two minutes indicates a vessel under sail. Be aware that other vessels will also sound this signal, e.g., vessels engaged in towing, fishing, pushing, and vessels restricted in their ability to maneuver.

Other sound signals:

— One prolonged blast is sounded by a vessel nearing a blind bend of a channel or fairway, or when departing a berth.

For other sound signals consult the *Navigation Rules, International-Inland.*

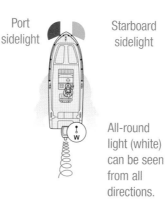

Light requirement for a powerboat underway whose length is less than 39.4 feet (12 meters).

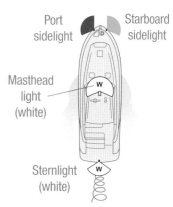

Light requirement for a powerboat (or sailboat using an engine) underway whose length is less than 164 feet (50 meters).

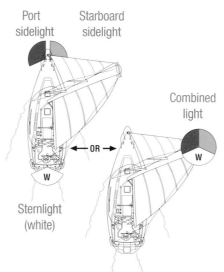

Light requirement for sailboats underway.

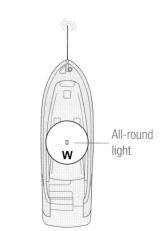

Light requirement for an anchored boat less than 164 feet (50 meters).

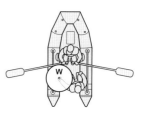

Light requirement for a boat being rowed: a flashlight is turned on in sufficient time to prevent a collision.

Glossary of Boating Terms

including radio phonetic alphabet (in parentheses)

A (Alfa)

Abeam - off the side of (at right angle to) a boat.

Aboard - on a boat.

Adrift - a boat drifting without control.

Aft - at or toward the stern or behind a boat.

Aground - a boat whose bottom, keel or skeg is touching the sea bottom.

Alternator - a device which generates electricity from an engine.

Amidships - toward the center of a boat.

Astern - behind the stern of a boat.

Athwartships - across a boat from side to side.

B (Bravo)

Back - a counterclockwise change of wind direction.

Bail - to empty a boat of water.

Barometer - a weather forecasting instrument that measures air pressure.

Battery switch - the main electrical cutoff switch.

Beam - the width of a boat at its widest point.

Bear away - to fall off, turn away from the wind.

Bearing - the direction from one object to another expressed in compass degrees.

Below - the area of a boat beneath the deck.

Berth - 1. the space in which you park your boat. 2. a bed on a boat.

Bight - a loop in a line.

Bilge - the lowest part of a boat's interior, where water will collect.

Bimini - a sun awning used to cover the cockpit or flying bridge.

Bitter end - the end of a line.

Block - a pulley on a boat.

Boat hook - a pole with a hook on the end used for grabbing hold of a mooring or retrieving something that has fallen overboard.

Bottom - 1. the underside of a boat. 2. the land under the water.

Bow - the forward part of a boat.

Bow line (BOW - line) - a line running from the bow of a boat to the dock or mooring.

Bowline (BOE-lin) - a knot designed to make a loop that will not slip and can be easily untied.

Breast line - a short dockline running perpendicular from the beam (at mid-length) of a boat to the dock.

Broach - a sudden, uncontrolled and powerful turn when running down a large wave. The boat will also roll on its side and in extreme situations could capsize.

Bulkhead - a wall that runs athwartships on a boat, usually providing structural support to the hull.

Bunk - see berth, definition #2

Buoy - a floating mooring ball or navigation mark.

Buoyancy - the ability of an object to float.

C (Charlie)

Cabin - the interior of a boat.

Can - an odd-numbered, green buoy marking the left side of a channel as you return from seaward.

Capsize - to turn a boat over on its side or upside down and not return to its upright position.

Cast off - to release a line when leaving a dock or mooring.

Cavitation - vaporized bubbles disrupt water flow on the propeller blades causing loss of thrust and erosion of the blades' surface.

Centerline - the midline of a boat running from bow to stern.

Chafe - wear on a line caused by rubbing.

Channel - a waterway where the water is deeper than the surrounding area and is often marked by navigation marks.

Chart - a nautical map.

Chine - the sharp edge formed at the intersection of the topsides and bottom of a boat.

Chock - a guide mounted on the deck through which docklines and anchor lines are run.

Choke - a device for controlling the mixture of air and fuel for an engine.

Cleat - a nautical fitting that is used to secure a line.

Coaming - the low protective wall surrounding the cockpit.

Coastal waters - include the U.S. waters of the Great Lakes, U.S. territorial seas and those waters directly connected to the Great Lakes and territorial seas where any entrance exceeds 2 nautical miles between opposite shorelines to the first point where the largest distance between shorelines narrows to 2 miles.

Cockpit - the area that is recessed below the deck or gunwale in which seats and boat controls are located.

Coil - to loop a line neatly so it can be stored.

Companionway - the steps leading from the cockpit or deck to the cabin below.

Compass - the magnetic instrument that indicates the direction in which a boat is headed.

Compass protractor - a plotting instrument oriented to latitude-longitude lines on a chart.

Compass rose - the twin circles on a chart which indicate the direction of true north and magnetic north.

Console - a structure in a cockpit or inside a boat on which the boat controls and instruments are located.

Course - the direction in which a boat is steered.

Crew - anyone on board who helps the operator (person in command) with handling the boat.

Crosscurrent - the direction that is perpendicular (at 90 degrees) to the direction of the horizontal movement of water.

Crosswind - when the wind direction is perpendicular (at 90 degrees) to a boat's course or its centerline.

Current - the horizontal movement of water caused by tides, wind and other forces.

D (Delta)

Deck - the mostly flat surface area on top of a boat.

Deck plate - a circular plate installed at openings in a deck and fitted with a threaded watertight cap if connected to fill lines for fuel or water tanks or pumpout lines for holding tanks.

Diameter (propeller) - the dimension of the circle made by the rotation of the tip ends of the propeller blades.

Dinghy - a small boat that can be rowed or sailed.

Displacement - the weight of a boat; therefore the amount of water it displaces.

Dividers - an instrument used for measuring distances or coordinates on a chart.

Dock - 1. a structure to which a boat can be tied. 2. the act of bringing a boat to rest alongside the structure.

Dockline - a line used to secure a boat to a dock.

Dodger - a canvas shield in front of the cockpit of some boats that is designed to protect people from spray.

Downcurrent - see downstream.

Downstream - in the same direction that the horizontal movement of water is flowing toward.

Downwind - away from the direction of the wind.

Draft - the vertical distance from the water's surface to the deepest point on a boat.

E (Echo)

Ease - to let out a line.

Ebb - an outgoing tide.

EPIRB - Emergency Position Indicating Radio Beacon

F (Foxtrot)

Fairway - the center of a channel.

Fall off - see head down.

Fast - secured.

Fathom - a measurement of the depth of water. One fathom equals six feet.

Fender - a flexible cylindrical or spherical object used to protect the sides of a boat when coming in contact with a dock or another boat.

Fitting - a piece of nautical hardware.

Flake - to lay out a line on deck using large loops to keep it from becoming tangled.

Flood - an incoming tide.

Float plan - an itinerary of your intended trip, left with a responsible party onshore.

Float switch - a switch for an electric bilge pump that is activated when water raises a floatable lever to a certain level.

Following sea - waves hitting the boat from astern.

Fore - forward.

Forepeak - a storage area in the bow (below the deck).

Forward - toward the bow.

Fouled - tangled.

Freeboard - the height of a hull above the water's surface.

G (Golf)

Gear - generic term for boating equipment.

Gearshift - the control that changes the direction of an engine and its propulsion system (propeller or jet drive) from neutral to forward or reverse.

Give-way vessel - the vessel required to give way to another vessel when they may be on a collision course.

Ground tackle - the anchor and rode (chain and line).

Gunwale (GUNN-nle) - the top edge of the topsides.

Gust - an increase in wind speed for a short duration.

H (Hotel)

Hard over - to turn the tiller or wheel as far as possible in one direction.

Hatch - a large covered opening in a deck or the top of a cabin.

Haul in - to tighten a line.

Head - the bathroom or marine toilet on a boat.

Heading - the direction of the boat expressed in compass degrees.

Head down - to change course away from the wind.

Head off - see head down.

Head up - to change course toward the wind.

Headway - progress made in the forward direction.

Heave - to throw.

Heavy weather - strong winds and large waves.

Heel - the sideways lean of a boat caused by torque from the propeller, side force from the rudder (when turning) or wind.

Helm - the tiller or wheel.

Helmsman - the person who drives a boat.

Holding ground - the sea bottom used to hold a anchor.

Holding tank - a tank that collects sewage from a marine toilet (head).

Hull - the envelope of a boat formed from a number of surfaces such as bottom, topsides, transom, cockpit, deck, and cabin.

Hull speed - the theoretical maximum speed of a boat determined by the length of its waterline.

I (India)

Inboard - inside of the rail of a boat.

Inverter – a device that converts DC (direct current) battery power into AC (alternating current) electricity.

J (Juliet)

Jury rig - an improvised, temporary repair.

K (Kilo)

Kedge off - to use an anchor to pull a boat into deeper water after it has run aground.

Keel - a vertical fin running along the centerline of a powerboat's bottom to improve its tracking ability by reducing its sideways slip in the water.

Kill switch - a switch that shuts off the engine and is activated by the release of an end of a cord from a button or an ignition switch.

King spoke - a marker on the steering wheel which indicates when the rudder is centered.

Knot - one nautical mile per hour.

L (Lima)

Land breeze - a wind that blows from land toward the sea.

Lash - to tie down.

Lazarette - a storage compartment accessed through the deck, usually located in the stern.

Lee shore - the shore to which the wind is blowing.

Leeward (LEW-erd) - the direction away from the wind (where the wind is blowing to).

Leeward side - the side of a boat that is away from the wind.

Leeway - sideways slippage of a boat in a direction away from the wind.

Left-hand (propeller) - a propeller that rotates counterclockwise in forward gear when viewed from astern (behind).

Lifeline - plastic coated wire, supported by stanchions, around the outside of a deck to help prevent people from falling overboard.

Lifesling - a floating collar, which doubles as a hoisting sling, is attached to the boat by a length of floating line and is used to retrieve a victim from the water.

Line - a nautical rope.

List - the sideways lean of a boat caused by more weight (i.e., people, equipment, fuel) on one side.

Lubber's line - a small post in a compass used to help determine a course or a bearing.

Lull - a decrease in wind speed for a short duration.

M (Mike)

Magnetic - in reference to magnetic north rather than true north.

Marlinspike - a pointed tool used to loosen knots.

Master switch - see battery switch.

Mayday call - the internationally recognized distress signal for a life-threatening emergency.

Mooring - a permanently anchored buoy to which a boat can be tied.

Marine Sanitation Device (MSD) - a marine toilet system that treats or stores the effluent to meet the requirements of the Clean Water Act.

N (November)

Nautical mile - a distance of 6076 feet, equaling one minute of the earth's latitude.

Navigation Aids - include beacons and buoys as well as lighted ones that are used to determine a boat's position or safe course, or to warn of dangers or obstructions.

Navigation lights - lights (i.e., sidelights, sternlight, masthead light, etc.) that are used to identify watercraft and help avoid collisions when operating from sunset to sunrise and during restricted visibility.

Navigation plan - includes compass headings, distances and estimated times to help you determine your boat's position or find your way during your intended trip.

Navigation Rules - laws established to prevent collisions on the water.

No-discharge zone - an area where the discharge of any treated and untreated sewage is prohibited.

Nun - a red, even-numbered buoy, marking the right side of a channel as you return from seaward. Nuns are often paired with cans.

O (Oscar)

Offshore - away from or out of sight of land.

Offshore wind - a wind that blows from land toward the sea.

Onshore wind - a wind that blows from the sea onto land.

Outboard - outside the rail of a boat.

Overtaking - a boat that is catching up to another boat and about to pass it.

P (Papa)

Painter - the line attached to the bow of a dinghy.

Pan-Pan call - the internationally recognized distress signal for an urgent situation.

Parallel rulers - an instrument with two rulers linked parallel by hinges used to plot a course.

Pendant - see pennant.

Pay out - to ease a line.

Pennant - a length of line used to attach a boat to a mooring.

Personal Flotation Device (PFD) - a life jacket or vest, life ring or other U.S. Coast Guard approved flotation device.

Piling - vertical timber or log driven into the sea bottom to support docks and/or secure docklines.

Pitch (propeller) - the theoretical distance that a propeller would advance in one revolution in a solid material (no slippage).

Plot - applying calculations to a chart to determine course or position.

Port - 1. the left side of a boat when facing forward. 2. a harbor. 3. a window in a cabin on a boat.

Power trim - hydraulic adjustment of the angle of outboard motors or stern drives while underway.

Prevailing wind - typical or consistent wind conditions.

Prop walk - the side force generated from the rotation of a propeller, which results in a boat's tendency to turn slightly instead of tracking straight.

Propeller - a hub with radiating blades used for propulsion.

Pulpit - a stainless steel guardrail at the bow and stern of some boats.

Pumpout station - a location where boats can empty their holding tanks.

Q (Quebec)

Quarter - the sides of the boat near the stern.

Quarter berth - a bunk located under the cockpit

R (Romeo)

Radar reflector - a metal object designed to be detected by other vessels' radar.

Rail - the outer edges of a deck.

Range - the alignment of two objects that can be used to indicate a channel or safe water or stay on course.

Raw-water - the water in which a boat floats.

Rhumb line - a straight course between two points.

Right-hand (propeller) - a propeller that rotates clockwise in forward gear when viewed from astern (behind).

Rode - line and chain attached to the anchor.

Rudder - the underwater moveable fin used to steer a boat.

Running lights - see navigation lights.

S (Sierra)

Safety harness - strong webbing worn around the chest and attached to the boat to prevent a person from being separated from the boat.

Scope - the ratio of the amount of anchor rode deployed to the distance from the bow to the bottom.

Scupper - a cockpit or deck drain.

Sea breeze - a thermal generated wind that blows from the sea onto land.

Seacock - a through-hull fitting with a valve.

Secure - make safe or tie a line to a cleat.

Sécurite call - an internationally recognized signal to warn others of a dangerous situation.

Set - 1. the direction of a current. 2. to dig an anchor into the sea bottom.

Shackle - a metal fitting to connect lines, wire, chain and other fittings.

Shoal - shallow water that may be dangerous.

Skeg - 1. a triangular fin on the centerline at the aft end of a powerboat's bottom to improve its steering and tracking ability. 2. a triangular fin at the bottom of the lower unit of an outboard motor.

Skipper - an informal term for a person in charge of a boat.

Slip - 1. see berth #1. 2. to cast off from a mooring using a doubled line.

Snub - to hold a line under tension by wrapping it on a winch or cleat.

Sole - the floor in a cockpit or cabin.

Solenoid switch - an electrical switch which shuts off the flow of propane.

Spring line - a dockline running forward or aft from a boat to a dock to keep the boat from moving forward or aft when used in combination with bow and stern lines, or to swing a boat when powering against it.

Squall - a short intense storm with little warning.

Stanchion - a stainless steel support at the edge of a deck which holds the lifelines.

Stand-on vessel - the vessel required to maintain its course and speed when it may be on a collision course with another vessel (unless the give-way vessel does not take action to avoid a collision).

Starboard - when looking from the stern toward the bow, the right side of a boat.

Steerage - ability to control direction of a boat when steering with a wheel or tiller.

Steerageway - minimum amount of boat speed needed to control its direction with a rudder.

Stem - the centerline or structural member on the forward profile of a hull running along the profile from the deck to approximately the waterline.

Stern - the aft part of a boat.

Stow - to store properly.

Sump - 1. a low point in the bilge where water from rain or leaks collect. 2. a tank where drain water from showers and iceboxes collect.

Swamped - filled with water.

T (Tango)

Tackle - a sequence of blocks and line that provides a mechanical advantage.

Throttle - a device for controlling the engine's revolutions per minute (rpm).

Tide - the rise and fall of water level due to the gravitational pull of the sun and moon.

Tiller - an arm used to steer a boat instead of a steering wheel.

Toe rail - a low rail around the outer edges of a deck.

Topsides - the sides of a boat between the waterline and the deck.

Transom - the vertical surface of the stern.

Trim - 1. the relationship of a boat's forward and aft orientation to the water's surface, i.e., level trim (same as designed orientation), bow up or down trim, stern up or down trim. 2. to adjust the angle of outboard motors or stern drives, i.e., to trim up or down.

U (Uniform)

Underway - when a vessel is not at anchor, tied up or aground.

Upstream - the direction that is opposite to the direction of the horizontal movement of water.

Upwind - toward the direction of the wind.

V (Victor)

Vee-berth - a bunk in the bow of a boat that narrows as it goes forward.

Veer - a clockwise change of wind direction.

Ventilation (propeller) - air from above is drawn onto the propeller blades disrupting water flow over the blades that causes a sudden loss of thrust and increase in engine rpm.

Vessel - any watercraft, including powerboats, sailboats, personal watercrafts (PWCs) or ships.

VHF- abbreviation for Very High Frequency, a two-way radio commonly used for boating.

W (Whiskey)

Wake - waves caused by a boat moving through the water.

Waterline - the horizontal line on the hull of a boat where the water surface should be.

White caps - waves with foam tops.

Windage - the amount of surface area of a boat that is presented to the wind.

Windlass - a type of winch used for handling anchor rodes (line and chain).

Windward - the direction toward the wind (where the wind is blowing from).

Windward side - the side of a boat closest to the wind.

X (X-Ray)

Y (Yankee)

Acknowledgments

While some of the principal contributors are highlighted below, a number of powerboat trainers were involved at various stages: Rich Brew, Tom Fisher, Guy Fleming, Jo Mogle, Ray Treppa, Heather Wakelin, Walter Wheeler and Rob Whitcomb. David Forbes merits special recognition for his contributions to the content and presentation of the material. During the book's development James Muldoon, Steve Colgate, Ruth Creighton and Susie Trotman have been a source of encouragement and support.

The U.S. Coast Guard's Office of Boating Safety is a primary source for much of the material for Chapter 8 Equipment & Requirements.

Writers

Dick Allsopp is a lifelong powerboater and sailor. A career naval officer and aviator, Dick retired as a Captain in 1988 after 32 years of service. His tours included Commanding Officer of VS 28 embarked in USS Independence; Navigator USS John F. Kennedy; and Commanding Officer USS Canisteo (AO99). Dick has been involved with the United States Sailing Association since 1992 as an Instructor Trainer, Regional Training Coordinator, National Faculty member and with the development of the Powerboat program. He is currently on the Training Committee, Vice Chairman for Powerboat Training.

Timothea Larr has served as Chairman of the United States Sailing Association's Training Committee and its National Faculty. As a naval architect she has been involved with the design of powerboats and sailboats. Timmy grew up using a variety of powerboats to commute to the local junior program and racing events around Long Island Sound, ranging from small outboard inflatables to high-powered twin screw inboards.

Designer

Mark Smith is a lifelong sailor, graphic designer, editor and illustrator, and is currently Creative Director for North Sails. Mark was editorial and art director for *Yacht Racing/Cruising* magazine (now *Sailing World*) from 1970-83, editor and publisher of *Sailor* magazine from 1984-86, and editor and art director of *American Sailor* from 1987-89. His works include design and illustration for the *Annapolis Book of Seamanship* by John Rousmaniere, published by Simon and Schuster.

Production Manager

Diane Cacase is a freelance graphic designer and production consultant. She is the former Production Design Manager at *Cruising World* and *Sailing World* magazines.

Principal Illustrator

Joe Comeau is an illustrator and graphic designer. He regularly contributes illustrations to *Cruising World* and *Sailing World* magazines and has been teaching graphic design for several years. Joe has had a love affair with the water since childhood where he grew up on Narragansett Bay, and whenever he can find the time, he is restoring his faithful Coronado 25' in Bristol, RI.

Illustrators

Kim Curran, Paul Mirto

Photography Credits

Dick Allsopp, Boston Whaler, Inc., EdgeWater Powerboats, David Forbes, Groco, Timothea Larr, Anne Martin, Medeiros Boat Works, Moran Towing, Ralph Naranjo, NOAA/Department of Commerce, Raritan Engineering, Mark Smith, Thetford Corp. and Yamaha

Index

rudder 19, 30, 39, 40, 42, 45, 64, 65
running aground 120-121
running lights (see navigation lights)

S
safe speed 95
safe water mark 110
safety equipment 69-73
    minimum required 73
scope 53, 54
sea breezes 25, 91
seacock 17, 18, 83, 84, 85
seasickness 114
securing boat 47
securite 82
sewage 74
shifting gears 38, 40, 66
shower 85
signaling equipment 70-71
slip
    leaving 40
    returning 46, 58, 67
sound signals 71, 96, 97, 98
soundings 101, 102
special purpose marks 111
speed regulations 75
spotter 117, 118, 119
spring line 46, 47, 56, 57
squalls 25, 89
state boating law administrator 68
steering
    bow thruster 31
    directed thrust 30
    prop walk 31
    rudder 30
    tiller 32
    twin-screws 31
    wheel 32
stern drive 18-19
stern thrusters 21
stern tube 19
stopping a boat 40-41
    coasting stop 41
    high-speed stop 41
    quick stop 41
stoves 85-86

alcohol 85
electric 85
propane 86
stuffing box seal 20
sump tank (see tank)
sumps 84-85
swamping 63, 116

T
tank
    fuel 15, 17, 27
    oil 27
    sump 85
    water 84
termination of use act 75-76
theft prevention 77-78
throttle control 10, 40, 64
thunderstorm 25, 89-90
tide 24, 91-92
    table 92
tilt control 10
toilet (see marine sanitation
    devices)
tools 15, 21
towboat rescue 122
towing 122-123
traffic separation schemes 99
trailer hitches 124-125
trailering 124-126
trim 34-35
trim controls 10
trim tab 34, 35
turns
    avoidance 43
    high-speed 43-44, 61
    low-speed 42
    pivot 42-43
    sharp turn 43
twin-screw maneuvering 64-67
    advancing throttles 64
    backing into slip 67
    docking 67
    gearshift controls 66
    leaving a dock 66
    pivot turn 65, 66
    sideways 66

turns 64-65
twist turn 65, 66

U
U.S. Coast Guard 25, 68, 69, 70,
    71, 72, 73, 74, 75, 76, 77, 81,
    118, 120
U.S. marking system 108

V
variation 104
ventilation (boat) 72
ventilation (propeller blade) 61
VHF radio 80-82
    antenna 80
    channels 25, 80-81, 118, 120,
    121
    communications 81-82
    weather forecasts 80
visual distress signals 70-71

W
wake 36
warm front (see front)
water jet (see jet drive) 8, 9
waterskiing 61-62
weather 87-90
    conditions 24, 87
    forecasts 24, 87
    map 87
western river system 112
wind 90-91
    onshore 25, 91
    offshore 91
    pressure systems 87, 90
windage 33
windlass 55

Please complete both sides of this form (including Survey on back side of this page) and mail to: US SAILING, P.O. Box 1260, Portsmouth, RI 02871-0907

✂

Answer Sheet

Name of Course _____   Course Location _____

Student's Name _____

Address _____   City _____   State _____   Zip _____

Phone (H) _____ (W) _____   E-mail _____   Fax _____

Gender (M) _____ (F) _____   Date of Birth _____   State-specific test (i.e. RI, MA, WA) _____

Instructor _____   INSTRUCTOR # _____

1. a b c d	18. a b c d	35. a b c d	52. a b c d	69. a b c d
2. a b c d	19. a b c d	36. a b c d	53. a b c d	70. a b c d
3. a b c d	20. a b c d	37. a b c d	54. a b c d	71. a b c d
4. a b c d	21. a b c d	38. a b c d	55. a b c d	72. a b c d
5. a b c d	22. a b c d	39. a b c d	56. a b c d	73. a b c d
6. a b c d	23. a b c d	40. a b c d	57. a b c d	74. a b c d
7. a b c d	24. a b c d	41. a b c d	58. a b c d	75. a b c d
8. a b c d	25. a b c d	42. a b c d	59. a b c d	
9. a b c d	26. a b c d	43. a b c d	60. a b c d	
10. a b c d	27. a b c d	44. a b c d	61. a b c d	
11. a b c d	28. a b c d	45. a b c d	62. a b c d	
12. a b c d	29. a b c d	46. a b c d	63. a b c d	
13. a b c d	30. a b c d	47. a b c d	64. a b c d	
14. a b c d	31. a b c d	48. a b c d	65. a b c d	
15. a b c d	32. a b c d	49. a b c d	66. a b c d	
16. a b c d	33. a b c d	50. a b c d	67. a b c d	
17. a b c d	34. a b c d	51. a b c d	68. a b c d	

MARKING INSTRUCTIONS
1. Use a No. 2 pencil or a blue or black ink pen only.
2. Fill in the response completely.
3. Make no stray marks on this form.
4. Please print clearly and legibly.

STICKER #

Please complete both sides of this form (including Survey on back side of this page) and mail to:

US SAILING, P.O. Box 1260
Portsmouth, RI 02871-0907

I hereby certify that this individual was not assisted in anyway or given any answers by any other person in order to complete this test.

_____
Instructor's Signature

_____
Name of test here

Survey

We periodically update and revise our books and products. Please help improve
Start Powerboating Right! **by filling out this survey and sending it to:**
P.O. Box 1260, Portsmouth, RI 02871-0907.

Do you operate a powerboat?   ☐ yes   ☐ no
    If yes, what is its length and type?
    ☐ less 16 feet   ☐ 16 to 26 feet   ☐ 26 to 40 feet   ☐ more 40 feet
    ☐ single screw   ☐ twin screw   ☐ outboard motor   ☐ stern drive
    ☐ jet drive   ☐ fixed prop

    If no, what kind of powerboat do you plan to operate?
    ☐ less 16 feet   ☐ 16 to 26 feet   ☐ 26 to 40 feet   ☐ more 40 feet
    ☐ single screw   ☐ twin screw   ☐ outboard motor   ☐ stern drive
    ☐ jet drive   ☐ fixed prop   ☐ don't know

Have you taken an on-water powerboat course?   ☐ yes   ☐ no

Why did you get this book?
    ☐ part of your course materials
    ☐ recommended
    ☐ saw it in a bookstore
    ☐ saw it on www.uspowerboating.com
    ☐ came with the boat
    ☐ Other _____

Please circle one for each category

	Excellent	Good	Average	Poor	Unsatisfactory
Easy to read	5	4	3	2	1
Concepts explained clearly	5	4	3	2	1
Completeness of information	5	4	3	2	1
Accuracy of information	5	4	3	2	1
Effectiveness of illustrations	5	4	3	2	1
Effectiveness of photographs	5	4	3	2	1
Relevancy to learning objectives	5	4	3	2	1
Overall book evaluation	5	4	3	2	1

What did you like about the book? _____

_____

_____

Do you have any specific suggestions for improving the book? _____

_____

_____

For more information on student operator or instructor courses, go to *www.uspowerboating.com*

Please complete both sides of this form (including Answer Sheet on back side of this page) and mail to: US SAILING, P.O. Box 1260, Portsmouth, RI 02871-0907